Fluency

The **READING PUZZLE**

Elaine K. McEwan
Kathie Ward Dobberteen
Q. L. Pearce

CORWIN PRESS
Classroom

For information:

Corwin Press
A SAGE Company
2455 Teller Road
Thousand Oaks, California 91320
CorwinPress.com

SAGE, Ltd.
1 Oliver's Yard
55 City Road
London EC1Y 1SP
United Kingdom

SAGE India Pvt. Ltd.
B 1/I 1 Mohan Cooperative
Industrial Area
Mathura Road, New Delhi
India 110 044

SAGE Asia-Pacific Pvt. Ltd.
33 Pekin Street #02-01
Far East Square
Singapore 048763

Printed in the United States of America.

ISBN: 978-1-4129-5823-3

This book is printed on acid-free paper.

08 09 10 11 12 10 9 8 7 6 5 4 3 2 1

Executive Editor: Kathleen Hex
Managing Developmental Editor: Christine Hood
Editorial Assistant: Anne O'Dell
Developmental Writers: Kathie Ward Dobberteen and Q. L. Pearce
Developmental Editor: June Hetzel
Proofreader: Carrie Reiling
Art Director: Anthony D. Paular
Design Project Manager: Jeffrey Stith
Cover Designers: Michael Dubowe and Jeffrey Stith
Illustrator: Karol Kaminski
Design Consultant: The Development Source

GRADES **K-3**

TABLE OF CONTENTS

Connections to Standards 4

Introduction 5

How to Use This Book 7

Put It Into Practice 8

CHAPTER 1
Learn Lots of Sight Words Well .. 9
Activities and reproducibles

CHAPTER 2
Read a Lot. 17
Activities

CHAPTER 3
Model Good Oral Reading 21
Activities and reproducibles

CHAPTER 4
Provide Oral Support for Readers 35
Activities and reproducibles

CHAPTER 5
Offer Plenty of Practice 51
Activities and reproducibles

CHAPTER 6
Phrased Reading. 77
Activities and reproducibles

CHAPTER 7
Assessing Fluency 81
Activities and reproducibles

References 96

Connections to Standards

This chart shows the national academic standards covered in each chapter.

LANGUAGE ARTS	Standards are covered on pages
Read a wide range of print and nonprint texts to build an understanding of texts, of self, and of the cultures of the United States and the world; to acquire new information; to respond to the needs and demands of society and the workplace; and for personal fulfillment (includes fiction and nonfiction, classic, and contemporary works).	18, 21, 48, 52, 67
Read a wide range of literature from many periods in many genres to build an understanding of the many dimensions (e.g., philosophical, ethical, aesthetic) of human experience.	18, 21, 67
Apply a wide range of strategies to comprehend, interpret, evaluate, and appreciate texts. Draw on prior experience, interactions with other readers and writers, knowledge of word meaning and of other texts, word identification strategies, and understanding of textual features (e.g., sound-letter correspondence, sentence structure, context, graphics).	9, 21, 23, 26, 35, 40, 41, 46, 48, 52, 55, 67, 72
Adjust the use of spoken, written, and visual language (e.g., conventions, style, vocabulary) to communicate effectively with a variety of audiences and for different purposes.	21, 23, 26, 35, 41, 48, 52, 55, 67, 72, 77
Use spoken, written, and visual language to accomplish a purpose (e.g., for learning, enjoyment, persuasion, and the exchange of information).	21, 23, 26, 35, 41, 48, 52, 55, 67, 77

Introduction

Dear Teachers,

When Dr. McEwan asked me to write about my experiences as part of this book, I was happy to relate how her reading strategies improved the reading skills of students at my school. Only 42% of our students were reading at and above grade level when I began my tenure as principal of La Mesa Dale Elementary School in La Mesa, California. Our students would never break out of the cycle of poverty if things remained the same at our Title I school. Reading, although an important aspect of the educational process, was not a focus. It was treated with a remedial flavor—putting Band-Aids® on small groups of students who were experiencing difficulties. We had great teachers who taught well and cared deeply for the students in their care, but we had no common, systematic focus.

We knew that change was needed and initially grasped at anything that was new. First, we taught multicultural education, hoping to build acceptance and tolerance among our culturally diverse population. Then, we emphasized conflict resolution to encourage respect, self reliance, and student ownership of what took place at school. None of these programs had any impact on student achievement. Fortunately, we attended a workshop on reading given by Dr. Elaine McEwan. She described the Reading Puzzle, which is a way of organizing and understanding reading instruction. The puzzle contains the essential reading skills that students need to master in order to become literate at every grade level. After looking at the puzzle, it was clear that we were missing some essential pieces. We had finally found our unifying vision.

The first component we put in place was an explicit phonological awareness program for kindergarten and first-grade students. At the end of the year, after teaching phonological awareness, the percentage of first-grade students reading at and above grade level improved from 55% to 88%. After that amazing success, we felt we were really onto something. We then focused on other areas of the Reading Puzzle. For example, we made sure our students were reading a lot and had a reading incentive program in which our goal was to read enough books that, when stacked together, would reach the height of the Sea World tower. Our students reached their goal, and we took the entire school to Sea World to celebrate. After decoding mastery, we focused on cognitive strategies so students could obtain a greater depth of understanding of what they were reading. We built a reading culture in which reading took place every single day of the school year.

After several years of incremental growth, we were close to having 90% of students reading at and above grade level, as measured by individual running records. Although we were excited, we still had a big dilemma on our hands. We were scoring very well on state-mandated tests but not as well as we should have with so many excellent readers. We did some additional research and looked more closely at students who were reading well above grade level on individual reading tests but were scoring at or below grade level on standardized tests. We found that we needed to work more explicitly on one piece of the Reading Puzzle that we had been put on the back burner.

We discovered that every one of our students who scored high on individual tests, and yet scored below grade level on standardized tests, also scored below grade level on reading fluency. Finally, we found both our problem and our solution. We began working on fluency with these students, and they, in turn, began scoring well on standardized tests. We ended up with 92% of students reading at and above grade level. We also scored extremely high on our state-mandated tests. We did so well that we became one of 96 National Title I Distinguished Schools in the country and were one of six schools in the nation to receive the Chase School Change Award from the Secretary of the Department of Education at Lincoln Center in New York City.

You, too, can use the Reading Puzzle to focus your vision and ensure you "teach them all to read." *The Reading Puzzle, Grades K–3* series is derived from Dr. McEwan's bestselling *Teach Them All to Read: Catching the Kids Who Fall Through the Cracks* (2002). It focuses on five of the essential components to successful reading instruction: Phonics, Phonemic Awareness, Vocabulary, Comprehension, and Fluency. Use this series as a guide to systematically put in place each of these components. This book is designed to support reading fluency instruction, a critical, but sometimes neglected piece of the puzzle in successful reading instruction.

Good luck with your reading journey!

Sincerely,

Kathie Ward Dobberteen, Retired Principal
La Mesa Dale Elementary School, La Mesa, California

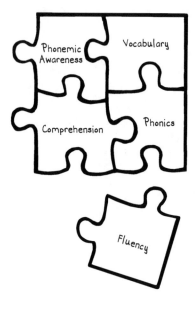

How to Use This Book

This resource book is designed to provide the strategies and activities that will help you develop your students' reading fluency. In order for students to reach grade level expectancies in the number of correct words they read per minute by the end of the year, they need frequent practice. Fortunately, fluency lessons do not take much time and are easy to prepare and teach. Fluency is simple to measure, and progress is readily apparent.

In my book, *Teach Them All to Read: Catching the Kids Who Fall Through the Cracks* (2002), I describe fluency as a frequently neglected piece of the Reading Puzzle. I explain several important methods for developing fluency and recommend that students should learn many sight words well and also read many different kinds of texts in lots of different ways both at home and at school. I also discuss a number of strategies that can improve fluency. These strategies can be categorized in several groups according to Timothy Rasinski (2003), including: 1) modeling good oral reading, 2) providing oral support for readers, 3) offering plenty of practice opportunities, and 4) encouraging fluency through phrasing.

Kathie Ward Dobberteen has taken my book, *Teach Them All to Read: Catching the Kids Who Fall Through the Cracks* (2002), and developed this derivative work, *Fluency, Grades K–3*, to make the research-based fluency activities accessible to all teachers. Each activity and lesson supports students' fluency development. In addition, samples of engaging passages, authored by Q. L. Pearce, accompany the lessons. Many passages can be applied with several strategies and utilized across grade levels. Passages were leveled utilizing the Flesch-Kincaid readability formula with minor adaptations. Passage levels were adjusted when passages contained key repeated multisyllabic terms and proper nouns (e.g., *Florence Nightingale*). These one or two key term(s) per passage, essential to meaning and recognized through configuration, sometimes dramatically skew the grade-level rating. Passage levels are coded at the bottom of each page, using the symbols shown below. Enjoy *Fluency, Grades K–3*. Happy teaching!

K = Kindergarten

2 = Grade 2

1 = Grade 1

3 = Grade 3

Put It Into Practice

What is fluency? The National Reading Panel determined that fluent readers can read text with speed, accuracy, and proper expression (Rasinski, 2003). Fluency is highly correlated with the ability to comprehend what is read (Fuchs, Fuchs, Hops, & Jenkins, 2001). In fact, measures of oral reading have been found to be more highly correlated with reading comprehension scores than were measures of silent reading rates in a sample of children whose reading skills varied across a broad range (Jenkins, Fuchs, Espin, van den Broek, & Deno, 2000). As students develop fluency in their oral reading, comprehension scores improve. According to Allington (1983), fluent oral readers, even with similar knowledge of the vocabulary and concepts in the text as their peers, are better able to understand what they read than are their dysfluent peers. Focusing too much attention on word recognition drains cognitive resources, impeding comprehension. Fluency enhances comprehension.

Fluent Reader　　　　　**Dysfluent Reader**

The National Research Council concluded, "Adequate progress in learning to read English (or any other alphabetic language) beyond the initial level depends on *sufficient practice to achieve fluency* [italics added] with different texts" (Snow et al. 1998, p. 223). The report also recommends that "because the ability to obtain meaning from print depends so strongly on the development of accurate word recognition and reading fluency, both should be regularly assessed in the classroom, permitting *timely and effective instructional response* [italics added] when difficulty or delay is apparent" (p. 7).

CHAPTER 1

Learn Lots of Sight Words Well

Students can improve reading fluency by learning lots of sight words well. Sight words are those words that, although originally phonetically decoded by the reader, have been read so frequently that they are now read fluently without attention to the letters in the words. Learning sight words usually takes some drill and practice to reach a level of automaticity. We know that practice in reading single words leads to increased fluency when those words are later found in text, and many words can be learned through simple flashcard repetition.

To draw attention to their spellings, more challenging words may need to be written several times after their introduction. Many enjoyable games can be played with flashcards, as long as the games are efficient and provide lots of word repetitions per session. Isolated word practice permits the teacher, parent, or tutor to build in more word repetitions per unit of time than can be achieved with repeated readings.

Read It! Read It! (Grades K-3)

"Read It! Read It!" is a homework program that ensures students learn required high-frequency words with the necessary level of automaticity. "Read It! Read It!" begins with sounds and letters at the kindergarten level. Once students have learned sounds and letters, the program moves on to lists of some of the most frequently used words in the English language. This homework program provides practice at home for the most important sight words and accountability at school to ensure memorization. Parents are a vital part of the program since they help students learn sight words appropriate for their grade level.

The word lists included in this publication were derived from several overlapping, research-based source lists, including: Dr. Edward Fry's *1,000 Instant Words* (2004), which includes words most commonly used for reading, writing, and spelling; Dolch's Basic Sight Vocabulary in *Problems in Reading* (1948), which includes words most commonly found in writing; Rebecca Sitton's *Spelling Sourcebook for Eighth Grade Teachers* (2002), which includes high-utility words needed for spelling; and words derived from current, practicing classroom teachers who based their lists on the needs of current students. The "Read It! Read It!" program helps to ensure that high-utility words are systematically mastered.

1. Send home a copy of the **Read It! Read It! Parent Letter reproducible (page 11)** to parents.

2. Start students with lists at the appropiate grade level on the **Sight Word Lists reproducibles (pages 13–16)**, and proceed through the lists sequentially. Back up or move forward if the lists are too easy or too difficult. Use the **Read It! Read It! Letters/Words List reproducible (page 12)** to introduce a new list each week. On the reproducible, write the letters and/or words students are working on each week before photocopying it and sending it home to parents. The letters and word lists have no duplicates. If you are starting the program in first through third grade, assess students' knowledge using the kindergarten list.

3. Ask tutors (paraprofessionals, parents, volunteers) to test students on a weekly basis on the letters or sight words from the previous week's list.

4. When students pass with a 100%, celebrate their achievement and provide a new list.

5. If students miss some words, highlight the missed words and send the list home again with a short note.

6. Chart the progress of each student.

7. Give students a sticker, star on a chart, or other recognition when they have mastered each list. Provide an award certificate when they have passed all the lists.

Read It! Read It!

	WEEK 1	2	3	4	5	6	7	8	9	10	11	12	13	14	15	16	17	18	19	20
Brian	★																			
Eric	★																			
Marta	★																			
Jose	★																			
Rosa	★																			
Sing	★																			
Tiffany	★																			
Bridget	★																			
Matt	★																			
Anna	★																			
Cory	★																			

Read It! Read It! Parent Letter

Dear Families,

"Read It! Read It!" is a great reading activity designed to help students recognize and read words with the highest frequency of use in the English language. In kindergarten, we will test students on letter recognition and ask them to provide the corresponding sounds of those letters. We will start with lowercase letters and then move on to uppercase letters, providing eight letters each week for study. Once letters are mastered, kindergarteners will start learning sets of six words, moving from the easiest high-frequency words to increasingly difficult words. Students in first through third grades will receive weekly word lists.

As your child masters each list of letters or words, a new list will be sent home. We ask that you work with your child on a daily basis for five to ten minutes each night. Make learning fun! Young students will enjoy writing letters and words in sand, pudding, or paint. All students will enjoy magnetic letters; writing with chalk on a small chalkboard; or writing each letter on a card, mixing them up, and reordering the letters. Older students will enjoy designing words with felt pens, creating word searches, and designing their own games for study. Be creative!

Once a week, a tutor (parent, volunteer, or older student) will test your child on reading his or her list at school. If successful, he or she will move to the next list. Your child will be recognized for each list mastered.

Thank you so much for your support. Let's have fun and "Read It! Read It!" together, ensuring that students enjoy mastering the alphabet and/or high-frequency words during their earliest years in school.

Sincerely,

_____

Read It! Read It! Letters/Words List

Dear Families,

Here is the list of letters or words that _____ is trying to learn to become a better reader. Please help by practicing the letters or words with your child each night at home for about 10 minutes.

Invite your child to try these fun ideas:

- Chant/clap each letter while spelling words aloud.

- Copy each word in a special color.

- Review words on flashcards.

- Use each word in a sentence.

- Trace words with a pencil or finger.

- Write words with an index finger in pudding, sand, or rice.

- Shape words with clay, wire, or cereal.

- Write words with a toothpick in clay.

- Cut out letters from magazines to spell words.

- Find the words in books at home.

If a letter or word is highlighted, it means your child has been tested and does not yet know it. Please remember that the more letters and words your child learns, the better reader he or she will become.

Thank you and happy reading!

Sincerely,

_____

Letter/Sound/Sight Word List

*LIST 1 a s o b m g x z

*LIST 2 t e c j n p w r

*LIST 3 d f i q u h l k

*LIST 4 v y A C L M Q S

*LIST 5 T B F O K Z W R

*LIST 6 D G I J E X Y U

*#LIST 7 H N P V ch th wh sh

LIST 8 see like my mom dad am

LIST 9 can a at the in I

LIST 10 it is and on play go

LIST 11 favorite because of love you to

LIST 12 that he for was are as

LIST 13 with his they be not from

LIST 14 have or by one all this

LIST 15 but what had there an your

LIST 16 were which their said if do

LIST 17 when will each about how up

LIST 18 we out them she many some

LIST 19 then so would other into has

LIST 20 could no make than first been

LIST 21 these more her two him time

LIST 22 its who now people made over

LIST 23 did only way find use may

LIST 24 down water long very after words

LIST 25 little called just where most know

*Students need to identify letter names and sounds.

#Students need to recognize sounds that digraphs make: *ch* as in *ch*eek, *th* as in *th*umb, *wh* as in *wh*at, and *sh* as in *sh*irt.

K

Sight Word List

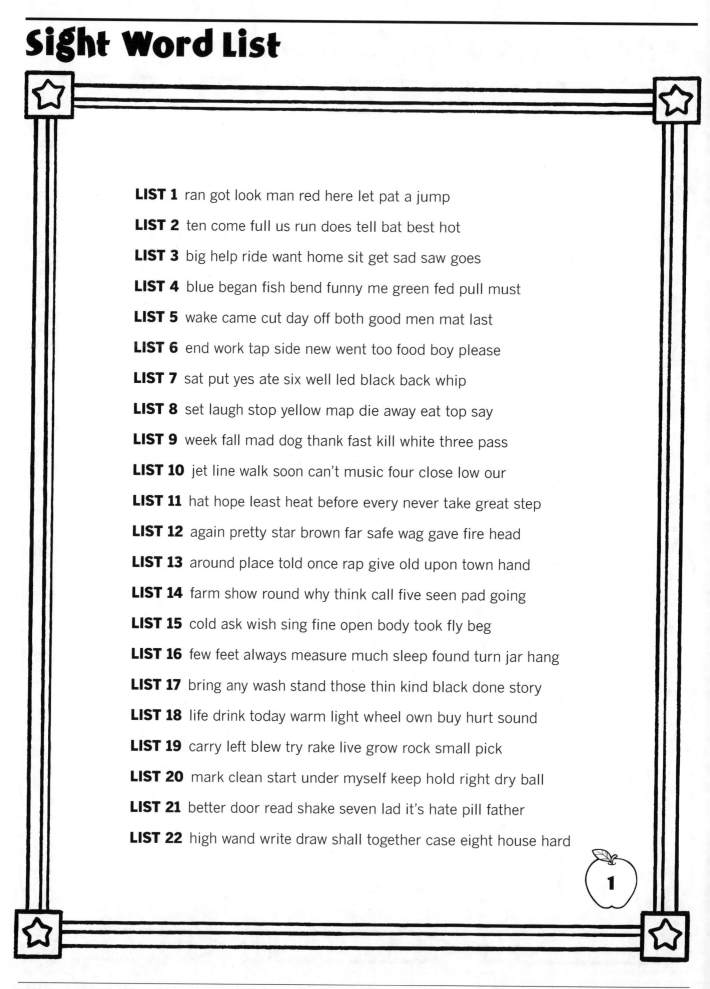

LIST 1 ran got look man red here let pat a jump

LIST 2 ten come full us run does tell bat best hot

LIST 3 big help ride want home sit get sad saw goes

LIST 4 blue began fish bend funny me green fed pull must

LIST 5 wake came cut day off both good men mat last

LIST 6 end work tap side new went too food boy please

LIST 7 sat put yes ate six well led black back whip

LIST 8 set laugh stop yellow map die away eat top say

LIST 9 week fall mad dog thank fast kill white three pass

LIST 10 jet line walk soon can't music four close low our

LIST 11 hat hope least heat before every never take great step

LIST 12 again pretty star brown far safe wag gave fire head

LIST 13 around place told once rap give old upon town hand

LIST 14 farm show round why think call five seen pad going

LIST 15 cold ask wish sing fine open body took fly beg

LIST 16 few feet always measure much sleep found turn jar hang

LIST 17 bring any wash stand those thin kind black done story

LIST 18 life drink today warm light wheel own buy hurt sound

LIST 19 carry left blew try rake live grow rock small pick

LIST 20 mark clean start under myself keep hold right dry ball

LIST 21 better door read shake seven lad it's hate pill father

LIST 22 high wand write draw shall together case eight house hard

1

Reproducible 978-1-4129-5823-3 • © Corwin Press

Sight Word List

LIST 1 above jacket umbrella year almost knew thought finish plan land

LIST 2 across key valentine lap age alone sister friend lose fireman

LIST 3 afraid kid still making air awake lawn until stay piece

LIST 4 lady yard march behind between leaf voice gone remember paw

LIST 5 banana lake afternoon neat below bicycle meal wait strong hour

LIST 6 band lamb afterward neck beside bigger mean sew herself short

LIST 7 cage kept against orange being caught meet yesterday himself should

LIST 8 calf mail bang meadow care chalk need young honk sign

LIST 9 camp nail bank woman careful change needle along itself someone

LIST 10 later named basket papa carrot deep ours also jumped through

LIST 11 daisy o'clock beat parade cart deer ourselves among knife twelve

LIST 12 dance often candle quiet dead den park angry learn upstairs

LIST 13 east page cannot quite evening ever except I'll leave without

LIST 14 enough pail card race feather feed kiss church rest writer

LIST 15 fair pancake dark radio since fourth answer biggest lesson yourself

LIST 16 family queen daughter same getting field rang chapter middle board

LIST 17 garage quick even sand having gift reach check might bite

LIST 18 gas heart fat sang held glass seek cheese mile bought

LIST 19 half example fear second invite hello seem asked news coming

LIST 20 hall sea special morning joke helped point desk nibble cough

LIST 21 hammer sail happy teeth king iron telephone notice nice cried

LIST 22 ill salt doubt uncle moment joy third everybody oven box

LIST 23 ink tag another visit large kitchen themselves everyone awful follow

LIST 24 inside tall lamp wagon common knee continue finger study fruit

2

Sight Word List

LIST 1 able everywhere probably accident main action lark team center object

LIST 2 aboard ladder act marble near lately tear travel organ annual

LIST 3 accept magic beach nearly adopt market tent chain person beyond

LIST 4 bare nap bead oat bean marry terrible deny pile already

LIST 5 barrel nation night heard picture neighbor untrue dew pint blanket

LIST 6 school however cape order became office used eleven pipe bless

LIST 7 bathe pack captain paid bedroom onion view elf reason question

LIST 8 cabbage package dare pain island palace whisper empty receive chase

LIST 9 cabin earth during suppose carpenter part whistle fellow shook cheer

LIST 10 canoe rack easy pair complete past whole felt shoot chimney

LIST 11 figure raft eaten raise cave path affair fence shore chirp

LIST 12 dangerous sack edge money ceiling anything city threw different product

LIST 13 eagle slowly fail rate death perhaps agree given shout enemy

LIST 14 easily tea faith season dentist rather ahead healthy sight engine

LIST 15 fact vase false secret either real alike clothes signal fight

LIST 16 factory wander general selfish feast really room heavy thick numeral

LIST 17 gain ugly gentle teach giant sentence ground guest flame covered

LIST 18 gather unfair happiest pattern certain several believe knob vine golden

LIST 19 handle yarn harm important hawk shade belong laughed violet good-bye

LIST 20 mother airplane idol untie image shape bench law alive hear

LIST 21 happen taxi early vegetable job sheet conclusion master willing decide

LIST 22 idle weigh hundred war journey shelf berry children wink heel

LIST 23 jam arrange kick weak kingdom shell contain matter wise helper

LIST 24 address usually ladies rough laid shirt cellar neither allow inch

3

Reproducible

CHAPTER 2

Read a Lot

Students must read different kinds of text in lots of different ways at both home and school. They should enjoy texts from a variety of genres and by a variety of authors. They should read text for real purposes, such as directions to build a model airplane or to bake cookies, as well as reading books that are compellingly interesting to them. Educators and parents help students become fluent by ensuring that a variety of text is readily available at home and at school.

What Does "Real Reading" Look Like?

"Real reading" takes place when students identify words independently, either by means of phonetic decoding or through the rapid identification of sight words. Although early literacy activities, such as language experience, are extremely beneficial for students, they do not count as real reading in the classroom because they do not provide the kind of reading practice that builds fluency. To become fluent readers, students must read a lot of text on their own. Young readers must process the text, practice unfamiliar words until they are stored in memory, and reread the same text repeatedly and orally to improve fluency.

Each student starts out reading slowly and haltingly, struggling to sound out words. With practice and over time, students become more efficient, transitioning to fluid, automatic reading that sounds almost conversational. Each student becomes a fluent reader on a slightly different timetable. However, there are far too many students who "get stuck" and do not become fluent readers because they do not practice enough real reading of continuous, connected text.

Books in Boxes

Just reading at school is never enough. Students must read voraciously, voluminously, and voluntarily outside of school as well (Shefelbine, 1999). We need to put books in students' hands every day. One method of making sure students have books readily available at home is to build an extensive classroom library. According to Trelease (2006), series books are motivational, as they make a pleasure connection with students, helping them want to continue reading. Reading many books of the same genre with familiar plotlines can also help build fluency.

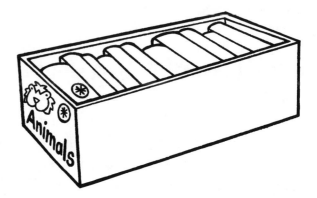

1. Establish a classroom library by purchasing clean, good quality books at low cost from garage sales, library sales, rummage sales, thrift stores, and book clubs. Consider asking families to donate their old books.

2. Organize books into categories (e.g., sports, animals, holidays). Books can also be arranged by author or series (e.g., *Curious George* books by H. A. and Margret Rey or *Clifford* books by Norman Bridwell).

3. Label and draw a picture on the front of each box, representing a different category.

4. Select a sticker for each box. Place the same sticker on the outside of each box and on each book in that category so students can replace a book in the correct box by matching the stickers.

5. Make a classroom library chart that has one library card pocket with each student's name.

6. Have students write the titles of the books they checked out on the index card in their library card pocket.

7. Tell students they must bring back one book before they can select another book.

How Many Decodable Books Should a Beginning Reader Read to Develop Automaticity and Fluency? (Grades K–1)

Reading decodable books in early primary grades is absolutely essential for developing reading fluency. Unless students are provided with a sufficient supply of decodable books in which to practice their word identification skills, they will not have the opportunity to become fluent readers. The following guidelines were adapted from the California Department of Education's *Criteria for 2002 Language Arts Adoption* (2001).

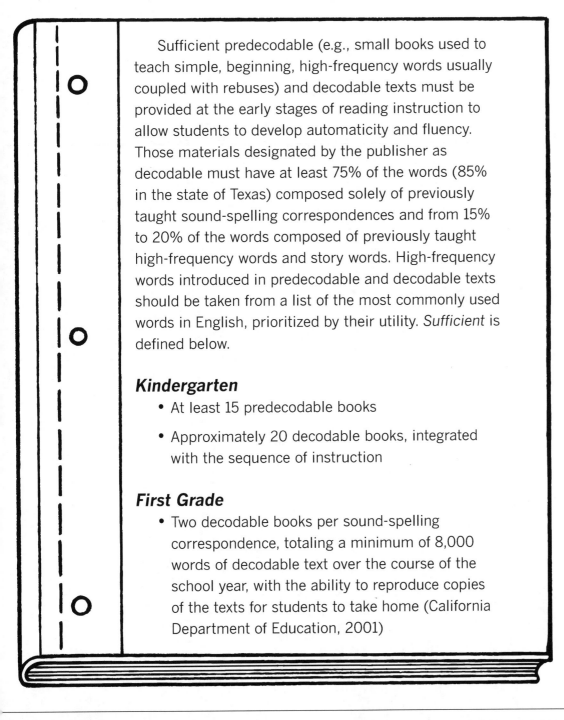

Sufficient predecodable (e.g., small books used to teach simple, beginning, high-frequency words usually coupled with rebuses) and decodable texts must be provided at the early stages of reading instruction to allow students to develop automaticity and fluency. Those materials designated by the publisher as decodable must have at least 75% of the words (85% in the state of Texas) composed solely of previously taught sound-spelling correspondences and from 15% to 20% of the words composed of previously taught high-frequency words and story words. High-frequency words introduced in predecodable and decodable texts should be taken from a list of the most commonly used words in English, prioritized by their utility. *Sufficient* is defined below.

Kindergarten

- At least 15 predecodable books

- Approximately 20 decodable books, integrated with the sequence of instruction

First Grade

- Two decodable books per sound-spelling correspondence, totaling a minimum of 8,000 words of decodable text over the course of the school year, with the ability to reproduce copies of the texts for students to take home (California Department of Education, 2001)

How to Organize and Use Books in Boxes

Becky Mortier, Third-Grade Teacher, Highlands Elementary, La Mesa, CA

A well-stocked classroom library is essential in any classroom. When students are surrounded by an array of interesting, magical, captivating books, they will be inspired to read. Nothing makes me happier than watching my students as they discover the classroom library for the first time each fall.

I began collecting books for my classroom library as soon as I decided to become a teacher. I would stand eagerly in line on Saturday mornings at library book sales and local thrift stores to buy used books in good condition. I was so thrilled with getting the books at such bargain prices that I collected books from kindergarten through fifth grade reading levels. This turned out to be a good decision, since second graders can be reading at any of those levels.

By the time I was hired to teach second grade, I had collected over 1,500 books! I wanted to arrange the books in a way that young students could manage themselves. I organized the books into different categories, placed each set in its own basket, and labeled each category with a small white sign. I chose a sticker to represent each category and placed it in the corner of each sign. I labeled each book in that basket with the same sticker, so the students knew where to return the book. This made maintenance of the library a breeze.

Students began to ask if they could take the books home. It is my personal belief that books belong in the hands of children, even if this means some books may not find their way back to my classroom. I created a simple checkout system in which the students were responsible for writing the title of the book on an index card and placing it in their library pocket. Most of my students took home books every week, and most of those books came back. The only rule was to bring back one book before you borrowed another. This kept the books circulating fairly regularly, especially the favorites.

My students made great progress in reading that year and in the years that followed. My classroom library has been up and running for five years now, often receiving new additions from garage sales, thrift stores, and book order bonus points. My students still take books home, and over the years I have lost very few. In fact, I now have students donating their old books to our classroom library on a regular basis. I'd venture to say that I have gained many more books than I have lost over the years.

CHAPTER 3

Model Good Oral Reading

Read-Alouds (Grades K–3)

Read-alouds allow students to see reading as emotionally powerful, motivate them to read more, expose them to multiple genres, assist them in exploring sophisticated words and text structures, and allow them to witness fluent reading (Rasinski, 2003).

Before Reading the Story

1. Introduce the book. Point out the title, the author, and the cover illustration.

2. Invite plausible predictions about the book's content.

3. Ask for text-to-self and text-to-text connections.

4. Conduct a "picture walk" through the book so students can formulate an idea about the book through the illustrations.

5. Talk about oral reading strategies that fluent readers use, such as pausing after words or phrases, using raised or lowered voice for expression, changing the speed of reading for emphasis, and reading a conversation with expression—as if the characters were speaking.

During the Story

1. Demonstrate the strategies in Step 5 above as you read the story.

2. Monitor the class. Watch students' body language to become aware of signs of boredom or confusion.

3. Allow students to see the illustrations when you are reading.

4. Occasionally articulate aloud what you are thinking as you read.

When the Story Is Finished

1. Confirm or revise story predictions based on what was just read.

2. Ask a few questions about the story: *How did this story make you feel? Has something like this ever happened to you? Does this story remind you of another book you have read?*

3. Ask students to describe several strategies that made the oral reading interesting.

How to Select Good Books for Read-Alouds

Reading aloud is a critical aspect of early literacy experiences and, for most students, lays a strong foundation for learning to read by nurturing language development as well as the acquisition of vocabulary and domain knowledge.

1. Challenge your students: Find books that are a little too hard for students to read on their own. This is a chance to introduce vocabulary and concepts that are somewhat beyond their reach.

2. Find books that appeal to you: Chances are, if you find a book that is appealing to you, you will make it interesting for your students. Age-appropiate nonfiction titles are great for capturing students' interest across a variety of topics.

3. Make text-to-self and text-to-text connections: Ask students how the concepts in the book might be related to themselves and to other books they have read. Making these connections helps students develop a context for the book and increases comprehension.

4. Talk to librarians, reading specialists, and colleagues: Other professionals also discover through experience what books most delight and instruct young students.

5. Discover books that have won awards: Some of these awards include the very well-known Caldecott and Newbery Medals, but hundreds of other awards are given every year.

6. Use *The Read-Aloud Handbook* by Jim Trelease (2006): This updated handbook contains an extensive list of excellent read-aloud books. The read-aloud list provides a synopsis of each book as well as the approximate "listening level" at which students can hear and understand the story.

7. Use the Internet to discover Web sites that have lists of recommended books. Most State Departments of Education have lists of this sort. A few others include: *www.rif.org, www. read2kids.org,* and *www.readaloudamerica.org.*

978-1-4129-5823-3

Teacher Modeling and Repeated Reading (Grades 2–3)

Teacher modeling and repeated reading works well when used with small groups of students working at the same reading level.

1. Make photocopies of grade-level-appropriate **Repeated Reading passages (pages 24–25)** and distribute them to students.

2. First, have students read the selected passage orally to a partner or an adult for one minute.

3. Determine the number of words read correctly and record the number.

4. Then invite students to read along silently while listening to an audiotape of the passage that models correct expression and phrasing. As an alternative, you can model fluent reading in lieu of the audiotape.

5. Prompt students to practice reading the passage until they are able to read it at a predetermined goal rate. Use a one-minute timer or a stopwatch to time the reading. Continue to record the number of words read correctly per minute to monitor improvement. See page 82 for suggested reading rates.

6. For the final assessment, have students again read the selected passage orally to a partner or an adult for one minute. Determine the number of words read correctly per minute.

7. Compare the number of words read correctly before practicing and words read correctly during the final assessment. Celebrate the students' achievements!

Repeated Reading

Florence Nightingale

Florence Nightingale wanted to help people. She wanted to be a (11)
nurse. She was born in Italy but lived in England. Her family was (24)
rich. Nurses were from poor families then. Florence's mother and (34)
father were angry with her. They wanted her to get married. (45)

Florence wanted people to have good health care. She fought for (56)
them. She took care of the poor people who could not pay. Florence (69)
went to see the soldiers. She heard that they needed help. She (81)
brought other nurses with her. She saw that there was not enough (93)
medicine. The hospitals were too crowded. There was no fresh air. (104)
She saw that no one kept the patients clean. The food was (116)
not good. (118)

Florence did her best. She could not save many soldiers, but (129)
she tried. She went back to England. She became very sick. She (141)
never fully recovered. Even though she was not well, she started to (153)
train nurses. She started a medical college for women. Her work (164)
in London was a success. She received many awards. She even (175)
received an award from the Queen of England. (183)

The school of nursing that she started is still there. Hospitals (194)
are named after Florence Nightingale. International Nurses Day is (203)
held on her birthday. (207)

Words Correct Per Minute: _____

2

Name _____ Date _____

Repeated Reading

The Greatest Little Horse

Figure was a small horse. He lived a long time ago. His father (13)
belonged to an officer in the American Revolution. A school teacher (24)
named Justin Morgan bought the pretty brown horse. The little (34)
horse grew strong. He was light, but he could pull heavy loads. (46)
He could pull a plow and a cart. He could carry a rider. President (60)
James Monroe once rode the gentle horse in a parade. Figure could (72)
run fast. He won a lot of races. He had strong legs and could jump. (87)
Figure's name was changed to Justin Morgan. (94)

People called his offspring *Morgans*. These horses are part of (104)
the history of America. Cavalry soldiers of the West rode Morgans. (115)
The strong horses pulled covered wagons. A Morgan named Black (125)
Hawk never lost a race. Today, mounted policemen often ride (135)
Morgans. The horse is also popular on cattle ranches. (144)

A Morgan horse is a pretty and intelligent horse. It is usually (156)
reddish brown or black. It is gentle and has kind eyes. A Morgan is (170)
good with children. Many people say that a Morgan will love and (182)
bond strongly with an owner. (187)

There is a statue of Figure in Vermont. He is called "the greatest (200)
little horse in the world." (205)

Words Correct Per Minute: _____

③

Read with Me (Grades K–3)

"Read with Me" is an opportunity for students to engage in repeated readings in the context of a read-aloud passage. You, the teacher, model fluent reading. Students become more fluent when they repeatedly read a second, shorter passage that orally intermingles with your story. When students engage with read-aloud passages, they are able to listen more actively, reinforcing comprehension skills.

1. Distribute copies of the "Read with Me" poem, **"I Can Tie My Laces" (page 28)** to the class. (Students will only have copies of the poem.)

2. As you read aloud the "Read with Me" story, **"New Shoes" (page 27)**, model fluent reading, using appropriate intonation, pacing, and expression.

3. Stop reading at the first asterick and point to students. Tell them this is their cue to read the poem in unison.

4. When students have finished reciting the poem, resume the story. When you encounter the second asterick, stop reading aloud and point to students again to cue them to recite the poem again.

5. Continue this procecure until you have completed the story.

6. Repeat with other related stories and poems on the **Read with Me reproducibles (pages 29–34)**.

978-1-4129-5823-3

Read with Me

New Shoes

Ryan sat on the end of his bed. He pulled on a pair of socks. His favorite shoes peeked out from under his bed. They were sneakers. They had long laces.* Ryan grabbed his left shoe. He slipped it on his left foot. He tied the shoelace and wiggled his toes a little.* Perfect! Ryan grabbed his right shoe. He slipped it on his right foot. He tied the shoelace and wiggled his toes a little.* Perfect!

Ri-i-i-i-i-p! One toe poked out through the top of the shoe.

"Oh, no," Ryan said. He ran downstairs.

"Look, Mom," he said. "There is a hole in my shoe."

Ryan wiggled his toe again so she could see.

"We need to take you shopping for a new pair," Mom said.

The shoe store was very big. It had rows and rows of shoes. There were boots and sneakers with laces.* There were sandals and sports shoes. There were work shoes and fancy shoes.

"Do you see a pair you like?" Mom asked.

"I like those," Ryan pointed to a pair of sneakers. They had long laces. He slipped on the left shoe. He tied the shoelace.* He slipped on the right shoe. He tied the shoelace.* Ryan wiggled his toes and smiled. Perfect!

Read with Me

I Can Tie My Laces

I can tie my laces, you know.

Over, under, and around just so.

I tie them in a knot,

Then I tie them in a bow.

Read with Me

The Robot Adventure

"Whoooooooshhhhhh!" John exclaimed. He held his toy robot in the air. It looked like it was flying.*

"Time to go to school," Dad called.

John finished his last bite of toast. He put the robot on the counter. John grabbed his backpack and raced to the car. He could see the robot through the kitchen window.

Mom opened the window. She waved good-bye to John. Not long after, Speckles the cat jumped on the kitchen counter. She sniffed the robot. She sniffed the air. She batted at the curtain with her paw. BUMP. The robot toppled out the window onto the grass! It rolled under the fence.* It rolled into Miss Parker's yard. Her floppy-eared dog was chewing on a ball. The dog dropped the ball and picked up the shiny robot.*

"Come on, Max," Miss Parker called. "Let's go for a walk."

Max opened his mouth to bark. The robot fell and bounced and rolled. It fell right into the swimming pool! It sank to the bottom.*

"What's this?" a young man said. He wore a shirt with words on the back that read *Sparkling Pools*. The man held a net with a long handle on it. He dipped the net into the water. He lifted the robot out of the pool. When he finished his work, the young man left the robot on a bench on the front porch.*

It wasn't long before Max and Miss Parker returned from their walk.

"This isn't mine," said the woman. She picked up the robot and looked at Max. "I'll bet this belongs to John next door," she said.*

"Woof!" Max barked in agreement.

John's mom was surprised when Miss Parker came to the door with the robot. She thanked her neighbor. She put the robot on the kitchen counter.*

When John came home from school, he ran to the kitchen.

"There you are," he said grabbing the robot. "Right where I left you!"

1

Read with Me
Silly Robot, Come Back Home

Robot flying all around.

Robot rolling on the ground.

Robot did not mean to roam.

Silly robot, come back home.

1

Read with Me

A Strange Dream

Flora tossed and turned in her bed. She was having a strange dream. In her dream she was in her classroom at school. Her friends sat at their desks. Flora thought it was strange that they all looked alike.* Everyone had red hair. Everyone wore a blue shirt. Flora looked up and down the rows of desks. There was a blue book on every desk. Everyone was writing with a blue pen.* Even the teacher had red hair and wore a blue dress. The teacher asked the students to read their stories. Each student stood and read. The stories were all about a summer vacation. They were all exactly alike.* In her dream, the world was a very dull place. Flora started to cry.

The alarm clock woke Flora. When she arrived at school, she walked slowly to her classroom. The dream had made her feel sad. She pushed open the door and peeked inside. Everyone looked different.* James in the front row had curly black hair and brown eyes. Shana had long blonde hair. Devon had red hair and lots of freckles. Flora liked bright colors, so she was wearing yellow shorts and a pink shirt.* Jordan had a big smile and a space between his two front teeth. The books and pencils at each desk were a rainbow of colors. Flora smiled. She was glad that the world was such an interesting place.*

Read with Me

It's Great to Be Unique!

We may not be exactly alike

In how we look or speak.

Let's celebrate our differences.

It's great to be unique!

Read with Me

A Special Gift

When Anna was trying to think of an idea, she would fidget. Today she wrinkled her nose, tugged on her ear, and tapped the table with her finger. She even curled up her toes, but she could not think of a good present for her mom's birthday. Tomorrow was the big day.*

Her dog, Shiloh, curled up next to her on the couch. She stroked his ear and tickled his tummy.

"Maybe it would help if I wrote down some ideas," she said to Shiloh. He wagged his tail. "I will make a list of all the things that make Mom happy."*

Anna found a notebook in her dresser drawer. She twirled a strand of hair around her finger and thought very hard. Mom liked the apple tree. On the first page, she wrote about a tea party she'd had with her mom. They had sat outside under the apple tree and enjoyed tea and cookies. Anna drew a picture to help her remember the day.*

Mom liked sunny days. Anna wrote about the time the family went to the beach. She drew a picture of her mom and dad and sister playing in the waves. She drew a picture of a sand castle and seagulls. Mom liked birds and dogs and dancing. Anna wrote a story about when they had made a bird feeder together. She drew a picture of them taking Shiloh for a walk in the park. She drew a picture of her mom dancing with her dad. Anna drew many pictures and wrote lots of stories, but she still could not think of a good birthday present.*

The next morning, Anna, her dad, and her sister sang "Happy Birthday" to Anna's mom. Her dad gave Mom a pretty, sparkly necklace. Her sister gave Mom some nice perfume. Anna felt very sad.*

"What is this?" Mom asked. She found the notebook Anna had left on the couch. Her mom read about the tea party and the beach day. She read about the bird feeder and walks in the park. She looked at all the pictures. When her mom finished reading, tears glistened in her eyes.*

"You must have worked very hard on this," she said. "It is an amazing birthday present. What a wonderful idea!"

She gave Anna a huge hug and a kiss. Anna looked at Shiloh. She was almost certain that he gave her a wink!*

Read with Me

A Gift Made with Love

Anna wants to give a gift

That she can be proud of.

The very best gift she can give

Is one that's made with love.

③

CHAPTER 4

Provide Oral Support for Readers

Choral Reading (Grades K–3)

How many of us remember a poem or a short speech that we memorized when we were elementary students? Although choral reading does not require memorization, it offers a wonderful chance for students to become familiar with some of the poetry and passages that are part of our heritage. Choral reading is especially valuable for dysfluent students because they can experience more challenging text without the risk of embarrassment.

1. Select a passage of 100–200 words (e.g., a poem, a famous speech, or an interesting passage) or use one of the **Choral Reading passages (pages 36–39)**.

2. Display the passage on an overhead projector or chart. Or, give one copy of the passage to each student.

3. Model the selected passage by reading it aloud.

4. Invite students to read the text aloud as a group with you.

5. Repeat the process numerous times over several days.

6. Practice the passage until students can read it with fluency, expression, and clear diction.

7. To celebrate students' success, invite a guest to hear the students perform.

Choral Reading

Apple Apple
Big Red apple
In a tree.
Do you wonder
What you'll be?

Apple tart,
Crisp and sweet;
Apple cider,
Juicy treat.

Big red apple
In a tree.
Apple pie
Is what you'll be!

Choral Reading

Ice Cream, Ice Cream

All: Ice cream. Ice cream.

Boys: Peach, lemon, cherry

All: We all scream for ice cream!

Girls: Mint and strawberry

All: Ice cream. Ice cream.

Boys: Chocolate in a cup

All: We all scream for ice cream!

Girls: Eat it all up!

All: Ice cream. Ice cream.
We all scream for ice cream!

(1)

Choral Reading

My Little Dog and Me

My dog and I
Went to the beach
To play along the shore.

We ran and ran
Across the sand,
And then we ran some more.

We splashed right in
The rolling waves
And paddled in the sea.

We had a very special day,
My little dog
And me!

2

Choral Reading

Three Wishes

Group One: If you had three wishes, what would you wish?
Group Two: I'd wish to have fins and swim like a fish.

Group One: If you had three wishes, what would you try?
Group Two: I'd wish to have wings like a bird in the sky.

Group One: If you had three wishes, what would be one?
Group Two: I'd wish to be fast as a horse on the run.

Group One: If you had three wishes, what would you wish for?
Group Two: I think I'd wish for twenty-three more.

Neurological Impress Method (Grades 1–3)

The neurological impress method (NIM) was originally used after World War II to teach brain-damaged adults to read again. NIM was first described in 1969 by Heckelman. This method can build confidence in the highly dysfluent reader (Heckelman, 1969). You can implement this strategy with students, or use a tutor to help (parent volunteer, older student, or paraprofessional).

1. Select an appropriate passage for the student to read. Interest is everything, so it is extremely helpful if the topic of the book or passage is of high interest to the student.

2. Sit next to the student, so you can read into his or her ear. (Some practitioners of NIM recommend sitting nearest the ear that corresponds to the hand with which the student writes or eats.)

3. Read in unison with the student, with your speed slightly exceeding the student's normal rate. This way, the student is forced to pay attention to whole words and sentences to keep up with you.

4. Track words by running a forefinger under them while you are reading.

5. After several joint oral readings of the text, allow the student to begin leading the reading while you maintain a secondary voice, supporting the oral reading.

6. Gradually give over the tracking responsibility to the student after repeated readings of the same text.

7. When a specific passage can be read at the selected target rate (usually a minimum of 85 words correct per minute), select a new, slightly more difficult passage.

978-1-4129-5823-3

Echo Reading (Grades K-3)

Echo reading allows students to practice small chunks of text so they can become fluent without the pressure of reading an entire passage. This strategy can be conducted with individuals, small groups, or the entire class.

1. Make photocopies of the **Echo Reading passages (pages 42–45)** and distribute them to students. Keep a copy for yourself as well.

2. Read aloud the first line of the text.

3. Prompt students to read the same line, modeling your example.

4. Have students continue reading in echo fashion for the entire passage. Gradually increase the amount of text that you and the class read at one time.

5. As you read, gradually increase the reading speed to push students to identify words more quickly.

Echo Reading

My Shadow

My shadow
Is a friend of mine
When I go out to play.
My shadow likes to come with me
When it's a sunny day.

My shadow
Is not happy
When gray clouds pour with rain.
My shadow hides on days like this
'til the sun comes out again.

My shadow
Likes to fly away
When I turn out the light.
It must be so! As I just don't know
Where my shadow goes at night.

Echo Reading

Five Little Ants

Five little ants
Marching by the door,
One got lost
Then there were four.

Four little ants
Climbing up a tree,
One dropped off
Then there were three.

Three little ants
Resting on a shoe,
One fell in
Then there were two.

Two little ants
Dancing just for fun,
One fell asleep
Then there was one.

One little ant
Found herself alone,
She turned around
And ran back home.

Echo Reading

A Stormy Day

Storm rolls in
Cold wind blows
The sun disappears
The storm cloud grows
Wind (Blows!*)
Cloud (Grows!*)

Sky is gloomy
Lightning flashes
Raindrops splatter
Thunder crashes
Lightning (Flashes!*)
Thunder (Crashes!*)

Storm clouds part
Raindrops slow
Sun comes out
A rainbow glows
Raindrops (Slow!*)
Rainbow (Glows!*)

*Children call out in echo in response to lead reader.

Echo Reading

Go Team!

The game begins. We have the ball.
Our team will race downfield.
The opposing team will try to block,
But (player's name) _____ will not yield.

The other team has got the ball.
We know that we can top them.
Because each time they try to pass,
(Player's name) _____ is there to stop them.

We have the ball. It's near the net.
Our team is on a roll.
Their goalie does not have a chance
When (player's name) _____ shoots at the goal.

Go team!

③

Kinderwrite (Grade K)

"Kinderwrite" is an interactive activity between you and your students. The passages that are produced in the process are students' own words and based on the curriculum area you are currently studying. Students are highly motivated to practice the passages because they have "written them themselves." Practicing these passages increases reading fluency.

At the beginning of the year, "Kinderwrite" stories are predictable. Choose the topic and then begin each sentence with the same predictable pattern (e.g., *I can see a _____.*). As the year goes on, stories become more complex (e.g., *I see a _____, and she is wearing a _____.*).

"Kinderwrite" takes three to five days to complete, providing many teaching and learning opportunities within that time.

Day 1

1. Guide student writing by thinking aloud. For example: *We have been learning about pumpkins. What could we say in a story about pumpkins?*

2. Encourage students to brainstorm about pumpkins, recalling information about the growth of pumpkins. Record their ideas on chart paper.

Days 2 and 3

1. Discuss the brainstorming from the previous day and sequence the ideas to decide what would be a good first sentence.

2. Guide students through the writing. For example: *Our writing today will use sentences that tell about how a pumpkin grows. We decided that our first sentence is going to be:* **We planted a pumpkin seed.** *How will we write this?*

3. Write the sentence composed by the class.

4. Ask a student to come up to the board to read a sentence, touching under each word as it is read.

5. Develop the "Kinderwrite" using the same strategies with each new sentence, thinking aloud as you go.

6. When the "Kinderwrite" story is finished, ask students: *What is our story about? What would be a good title for our story?*

7. Go back and have students listen as you read aloud the story to them.

8. Then have students read the story aloud as a group, while you touch under each word.

Day 4

1. Read aloud the "Kinderwrite" story from the previous day.

2. Ask individual students to come to the chart paper and point to and read words that they know.

3. Point out the strategies of good readers, using picture clues, context clues, phonetic knowledge, and so on, to figure out unknown words.

4. After all words have been identified, invite students to come up and read select sentences, using a pointer and correct tracking.

5. Choose two students who can take the story, read it, and draw an illustration at the top of the chart paper.

6. Display the story in the room so that all students can read it.

Day 5

1. Review the "Kinderwrite". Have students come up to track and read each sentence.

2. Provide individual printed copies of the passage in booklet form for each student to illustrate.

3. Direct students to track the passage and read it aloud to at least five listeners.

4. Remind students to ask each listener to initial the back of their booklet after listening.

5. Encourage students to take home their stories to read to their families.

Fluency Development (Grades 2–3)

The fluency development lesson is a combination of reading aloud, choral reading, listening to students read, and reading performance. This lesson should be implemented on a daily basis for several weeks, but it need not take longer than 15 minutes to complete each day (Rasinski, 2003).

1. Select a short, predictable passage of 100–150 words, such as the **Fluency Development passages (pages 49–50)**.

2. Make one copy of the passage for each student, or create a transparency for the overhead projector.

3. First, model reading the passage aloud using a variety of voices, including a dysfluent, unexpressive voice.

4. Then briefly discuss the different voices and why the unexpressive, staccato voice was unpleasant.

5. Solicit interpretations of the passage and clarify any difficult vocabulary.

6. Invite students to read the passage along with you. Repeat several times.

7. Organize the class into pairs. Have each student read the passage at least three times to his or her partner.

8. Remind partners to provide feedback, assistance, and support to one another.

Fluency Development

Our Home Planet

Earth is our home planet. It is a special place. It is far enough from the sun so we do not get too hot, but close enough to the sun so we do not get too cold.

The atmosphere is like a blanket around the planet. It has just the right mix of gases that living things breathe. It keeps dangerous rays of the sun from reaching us. The atmosphere lets in enough of the sun's heat to keep us warm, and it lets in the sun's light to help plants grow.

Another important thing on Earth is liquid water. Most living things need water. Plants soak water up from the soil. Animals drink water or get water from their food.

The Earth is a good home. We need to take care of it. We need to keep the air and the water clean. If we don't take care of our planet, who will?

2

Fluency Development

The World of Chocolate

Do you like chocolate? Did you know that chocolate grows on trees? It does. Chocolate comes from beans. The beans grow in pods of the cacao tree. There are many beans in each pod. The trees grow in Mexico and Central America.

Long ago, people dried the beans. They roasted them and ground them up. They mixed them with water and spices. They poured the mix back and forth in special cups. This made the liquid foamy. The drink was bitter, but it tasted good. The drink was for important people only. Many people loved chocolate. They even used cacao seeds as money.

Spanish soldiers learned about the tasty secret. They sent beans to Spain. The people there didn't like it at first. They tried to make it taste better. They added spices. They added sugar to the drink. Soon people everywhere loved the sweet chocolate drink. Then, about two hundred years ago, Joseph Fry figured out how to make chocolate into solid bars and candy. Chocolate bars were a big hit.

Today, there are chocolate cakes and candy. Chocolate is in pudding, ice cream, and drinks like milkshakes and hot cocoa. Chocolate is one of the world's favorite flavors.

3

CHAPTER 5

Offer Plenty of Practice

How to Choose Text for Repeated Oral Reading (Grades 1-3)

Choose a selection of about 50–100 words that is on students' independent reading level (the highest level at which students can read without assistance, with few errors in word recognition and with good comprehension and recall).

Time students' reading of the sample and note the number of correct words and the number of errors. If students take more than two minutes to read a passage or make more than five errors, the passage is too difficult. If students can read a passage at 85 words per minute with two or fewer errors, the passage is too easy. Choose a more difficult one.

If a passage is deemed suitable for repeated reading practice, then go over any errors that were made. Ask students to repeatedly read the chosen passage until they are confident in their reading. Encourage students to practice reading in the following ways: read orally to oneself; listen to an audiotape while reading along and then read orally without the tape; or read the selection orally to an adult or peer. Always take note of the correct words per minute.

Keep track of students' progress on a graph or chart. The goal is for students to improve their fluency when reading challenging material to at least 85 words correct per minute before moving on to a new passage (Gunning, 1998). See grade level expectancy of words correct per minute on page 82.

Paired Reading with a Peer (Grades 1-3)

Paired reading is one of the simplest types of reading activities and can easily be conducted in a reading group. This strategy takes very little preparation and yet is very effective in increasing reading fluency.

1. Have students read with a partner who is on the same reading level.

2. One student orally reads the passage three to five times.

3. The other student then reviews errors and evaluates his or her partner's level of fluency.

4. Partners then reverse roles and repeat the process.

Radio Reading (Grades 2–3)

In "Radio Reading," students are assigned selected portions of a text that will be used for shared reading, a read-aloud, or a lesson in a content area (Searfoss, 1975). This strategy is a great alternative to "round robin" reading.

1. Have small groups of students work together and prepare sections of a chapter to be read chorally.

2. Ask students to read their portion as many times as needed to develop expression and fluency.

3. More proficient students might read parts of the chapter solo.

4. Invite one student to be the announcer and read the opening and closing portions of the chapter.

Read Around (Grades 2–3)

"Read Around" provides an easy method for motivating students to read a passage of their own choosing until it is polished for a quick performance (Tompkins, 1998). "Read Around" can be a required activity or offered as an optional opportunity for students once or twice a week.

1. Ask students to choose a favorite poem, narrative text, or lyrics, or one of the **Read Around passages (pages 53–54)**.

2. Have students rehearse the passage until they can read it fluently.

3. Students then read the passage aloud to peers, a small group, or the entire class.

Read Around

The First Thanksgiving

We enjoy Thanksgiving Day on the fourth Thursday in November. We eat turkey, sweet potatoes, and cranberry sauce. The first Thanksgiving feast was based on the Pilgrim feast of long ago. In 1620, a group of Pilgrims left England. The Pilgrims wanted to live where they could be free. They set sail for America. The Pilgrims spent two months at sea. The trip across the ocean was hard. They didn't have much to eat. They were not used to being on a ship for so long. The ship was damp. It was not healthy.

They landed in America in winter. They did not know how to find food. They could not grow food. The ground was frozen. Many were already sick. Half died.

An Indian named Squanto helped the Pilgrims. He had visited England. He could speak English. He showed them how to survive the winter.

In spring, Squanto and his people helped the Pilgrims to plant corn. They helped them find other food. To thank their new friends, the Pilgrims invited them to eat. The meal included turkey, ducks, roasted corn, sweet potatoes, oysters, and cranberry sauce. The feast lasted for three days.

2

Read Around

John Bell Hatcher

John Bell Hatcher was a fossil hunter in the American West. He searched for fossils in Wyoming and other states. One day he met a cowboy who had found something strange. The cowboy said he found a big skull. He said the skull had horns as long as a hoe handle and eyes as big as a hat.

Hatcher wanted to see for himself. He went to the place the cowboy described. He discovered a huge, horned skull. He sent the skull to a scientist named Marsh. Marsh knew it was a triceratops. Triceratops was a large, plant-eating dinosaur. It had a huge frill around its neck. It had long powerful horns. Its name means "three-horned face."

Hatcher found fifty more animal fossils. He also found tiny mammal teeth. Marsh said the teeth were rare, but Hatcher found a lot of them. He didn't do it alone. He had some tiny helpers. He found the teeth in the anthills of western red carpenter ants. As the ants dug out their nests, they would pile up small stones around the opening to protect it. Luckily for Hatcher, many of the stones turned out to be the teeth he was searching for.

3

Talking for Two (Grades 1-3)

Short plays for two students provide motivating practice that takes less time than preparing for a complete "Reader's Theater."

1. Make photocopies of the **Talking for Two scripts (pages 56-62)**.

2. Assign each student a part in the play.

3. Have students repeatedly practice their parts to improve delivery.

4. Invite students to perform their play for the rest of the class.

Reader's Theater (Grades 1-3)

"Reader's Theater" helps text come alive as students take on the roles presented in short plays. This method of repeated reading enables students to participate in reading a play without the props, scenery, and endless rehearsal. Students do not memorize lines or wear costumes. They just repeatedly read their parts orally in preparation for the "performance" (Opitz & Rasinski, 1998).

1. In preparation, gather tapes of old radio shows. The library and the Internet are great sources for recordings.

2. Play some of the recordings and discuss how powerful text can be when read fluently and with appropriate expression.

3. Select one of the **Reader's Theater scripts (pages 63-66)**. Assign each student a part in the play.

4. Have students repeatedly practice their individual parts to improve their delivery.

5. Encourage students to practice reading the script as a group.

6. Provide an opportunity for students to perform the play for invited guests.

Talking for Two

The Best Pets

Characters: Dog and Cat
Setting: *In the Yard*

Dog: I am the best pet.
Cat: I am the best pet.
Dog: People like me best.
Cat: People like me best.

Dog: I have a happy bark.
Cat: I have a fine meow.
Dog: I can wag my tail.
Cat: I can purr.

Dog: I can run faster than a cat.
Cat: I can climb higher than a dog.
Dog: I can bounce a ball.
Cat: That sounds like lots of fun.

Dog: It is fun. What can you do?
Cat: I can toss a stuffed mouse.
Dog: That sounds like lots fun.
Cat: It is fun.

Dog: People pet my soft fur.
Cat: People pet my soft fur, too.
Dog: People like both of us!
Cat: We are the best pets!

1

Talking for Two

Pretty Colors

Reader 1: I like to paint. Blue looks the best.
Reader 2: I like to paint. Red is brighter than the rest.
Both Readers:

Mix them up in a cup. What color will it be?
They make deep purple. Can you see?

Reader 1: I like to paint. Yellow looks the best.
Reader 2: I like to paint. Blue is softer than the rest.
Both Readers:

Mix them up in a cup. What color will it be?
They make grass green. Can you see?

Reader 1: I like to paint. Red looks the best.
Reader 2: I like to paint. Yellow is sunnier than the rest.
Both Readers:

Mix them up in a cup. What color will it be?
They make cheerful orange. Can you see?

Talking for Two

How the Garden Grows

Both Gardeners:

We're planting a garden in the sun.
We hope it grows for everyone.

Gardener 1: I have the garden spade.
I'll dig deep down.

Gardener 2: I have the seeds.
I'll put them safely in the ground.

Gardener 1: We'll grow peppers.
We'll grow chard.

Gardener 2: We'll grow tomatoes
In this yard.

Gardener 1: Here's the corn seed
That I chose.

Gardener 2: We will plant it
In long, neat rows.

Gardener 1: I have the garden hose.
I'll water every day.

Gardener 2: We can take turns.
What do you say?

Both Gardeners:

We're planting a garden in the sun.
We hope it grows for everyone.

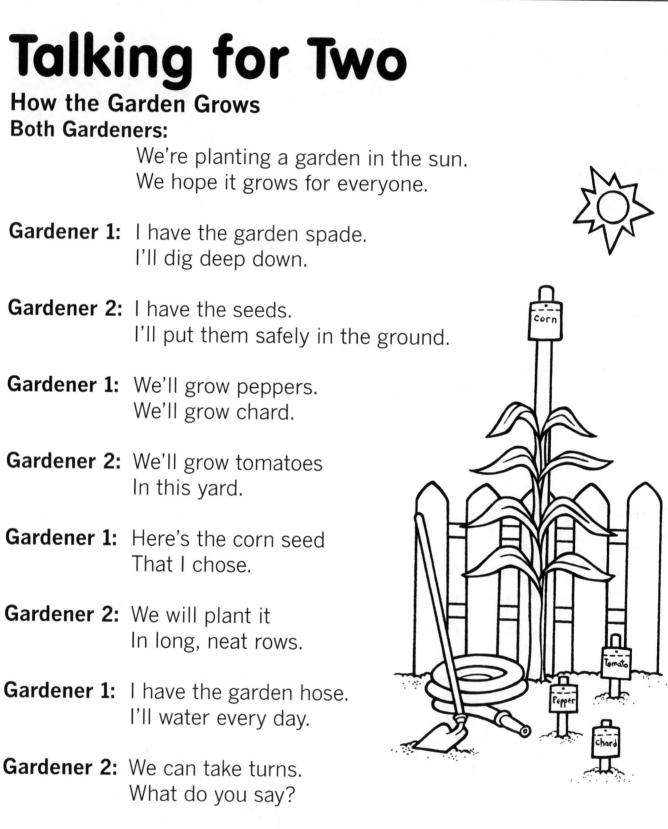

2

Reproducible   978-1-4129-5823-3 • © Corwin Press

Talking for Two

The Biggest Surprise

Characters: Thomas and Sara

Setting: *In the School Auditorium*

Thomas: I'm very excited. Today we will see who won the school art contest.

Sara: I love to draw and paint. I hope I won a prize.

Thomas: Sara, I think you are the best artist in our class. I know you will win.

Sara: Thank you, Thomas. I'm glad we can sit in the front row so we can see all of the drawings and paintings.

Thomas: I like that picture of the brown horse. *(Thomas points.)*

Sara: I like your picture of a snowman.

Thomas: Look, our teacher is ready to announce the winners.

Sara: There are many people here. It is nice that so many parents have come.

Thomas: I'm glad my mother and father are here. I hope I win a prize so they will be proud of me.

Sara: I wish my mother or father could be here, but they have to work today.

Thomas: The teacher gave the picture of the horse a green ribbon.

Sara: I'm glad that it won.

Thomas: She gave my painting a red ribbon!

Sara: I'm happy for you. I know you worked very hard.

Thomas: Sara, the teacher gave your painting the blue ribbon!

Sara: I am so surprised! I won first place!

Thomas: Why do you look sad?

Sara: I wish my mother and father could see my ribbon.

Thomas: They can! They are both sitting over there in the back row. *(Thomas points.)*

Sara: That is the biggest and best surprise of all!

2

Talking for Two

The Bake Sale

Characters: Jorge and Amanda
Setting: *At the Sports Park*

Amanda: Hello, Jorge. Are you ready for our bake sale today?

Jorge: Yes, I am. I hope we can make some money to help buy new soccer uniforms for our team.

Amanda: It is a sunny day, so my dad put the table in a shady spot.

Jorge: That's great! My mom made lots of treats for us to sell.

Amanda: My family made lots of treats, too.

Jorge: What should we do first?

Amanda: Can you carry these boxes, or do you need help?

Jorge: I can pick them up by myself because they are very light.

Amanda: There are eight clean trays on the table. We can put all of the cookies and cakes on the trays.

Jorge: This box is full of chocolate chip cookies. They are my favorite, and they are still warm.

Amanda: There are sixty cookies, so I will put them on the tray in six rows with ten in each row.

Jorge: Here is a chocolate cake. I like cake even better than cookies.

Amanda: Be careful, and don't let it fall.

Jorge: Don't worry, I won't drop it.

Amanda: These cupcakes look tasty, but they are small.

Jorge: We can put them all on one tray.

Amanda: I brought paper and markers so that we can make a sign for our sale.

Jorge: I'll draw a picture of a soccer player on the sign.

Amanda: I think everything is ready.

Jorge: It looks perfect!

3

Talking for Two

Grasshopper and Ant
Characters: Narrator 1 and Grasshopper, Narrator 2 and Ant
Setting: *A field*

Narrator 1:   On a lovely summer day, the grasshopper played in the field.

Narrator 2:   He saw an ant carrying grain to her nest.

Grasshopper: Hello, Ant. I'm lonely. Come and play with me. We can sing a tune.

Ant: I don't have time to play. Winter is coming, and I have to store my food. You should do the same.

Grasshopper: Winter is a long time, off so I'll worry about food later.

Narrator 1:   On a crisp fall day, the grasshopper played in the field.

Narrator 2:   He saw Ant carrying corn to her nest.

Grasshopper: Hello, Ant. It's such a lovely day. Come relax for a while. We can sing a tune.

Ant: I'll relax when my work is done. Winter is coming, and I have to store my food. You should, too.

Grasshopper: There is plenty of time. I'll work soon.

Narrator 1:   When the first snow came, Grasshopper could not find food. He was cold and hungry.

Narrator 2:   Then Grasshopper saw Ant. She was near her nest, and she looked plump and happy.

3

Talking for Two

Grasshopper and Ant (cont.)

Grasshopper: Dear friend, you have plenty of corn and grain. I'm so
hungry. Will you share with me?

Ant: I only have enough to feed my family through
the winter.

Narrator 1: Ant shook her head sadly. She felt sorry for
Grasshopper.

Ant: I can give you a little, but you will have to make it last.
You will be hungry this winter.

Grasshopper: You are a good friend. I have learned my lesson!

Narrator 2: Grasshopper made it through the winter. In the spring,
he found lots of food. In the summer, he saw Ant
carrying grain.

Grasshopper: Hello, Ant. Let's carry grain together.

Ant: I'd love to. I'm glad to see that this year you are singing
a different tune!

3

Reader's Theater

The Three Pigs

Characters: Mother, Big Pig, Middle Pig, Little Pig, Wolf
Setting: *A Forest*

Mother:	We need a bigger house. Who will build it?
Big Pig:	I will build it. I will build it with lots of straw.
Middle Pig:	I will build it. I will build it with bunches of sticks.
Little Pig:	I will build it. I will build it with strong bricks.
Big Pig:	Bricks are too heavy. I finished my straw house.
Mother:	Your house is light.
Middle Pig:	Bricks are too ugly. I finished my stick house.
Mother:	Your house is pretty.
Little Pig:	Bricks are strong. I finished my brick house.
Mother:	Your house is sturdy.
Big Pig:	Now I will bake a tasty cake.
Middle Pig:	Now I will bake a yummy pie.
Little Pig:	Now I will bake crunchy cookies.
Wolf:	I smell cake. I will huff and puff, and I will blow the straw house down! I will gobble up the cake.

Reader's Theater

The Three Pigs (cont.)

Big Pig: Run! Run to the brick house!

Wolf: I smell a pie. I will huff and puff, and I will blow the stick house down! I will gobble up the pie.

Middle Pig: Run! Run to the brick house!

Wolf: I smell cookies. I will huff and puff, and I will blow the brick house down! I will gobble up the cookies.

Big Pig: The bricks are too strong for the wolf.

Middle Pig: The bricks are too sturdy for the wolf.

Wolf: I give up!

Mother: We are safe!

Little Pig: Who wants a cookie?

Reader's Theater

A Visit to the Farm
Characters: Farmer, Brian, Lisa, Jackie
Setting: *A Small Farm*

Farmer: Hello, children. I'm glad you have come to visit. Who has been to a farm before?

Brian: I have been to a farm. My uncle works on a farm where they raise chickens. We always have lots of fresh eggs.

Lisa: I have been to a farm. My grandparents live near a farm where corn grows tall in long rows.

Jackie: I have never been to a farm. Do you have cows and pigs here? Do you have horses? I would like to meet all the animals.

Farmer: There are many kinds of animals here, big and small. Let's see how many you can find.

Brian: I see a cow with her baby calf. Milk comes from cows.

Lisa: I see a goat. Some people like cheese made from goat's milk.

Jackie: I see a horse. I know that a horse is for riding.

Farmer: Not all animals on a farm are big. Can you find some tiny animals that are important on a farm?

Brian: I see a bee buzzing in the air. Bees make honey.

Farmer: That's right, and bees carry pollen from flower to flower.

Lisa: I see an earthworm in the garden. My dad says that earthworms help plants to grow.

Farmer: That is because earthworms make the soil better.

Jackie: I see a spider by the barn. Some insects bite animals or eat plants. A spider can catch lots of insects in its web.

Brian: The farmer was right. Farm animals are big and small!

Reader's Theater

The Mystery of the Missing Notes
Characters: Mrs. Lopez, Robert, James, Maggie
Setting: *A Classroom*

Mrs. Lopez: Is everyone ready for vocabulary practice?

Robert: I have my vocabulary cards.

James: I have mine, too.

Maggie: Mrs. Lopez, I can't find my vocabulary cards.

Mrs. Lopez: When did you last see them?

Maggie: I put them on my desk when we finished working on our science experiments. They were clipped together with a big paper clip.

Robert: Did you check under your books?

Maggie: I looked under my books, and the cards are not there.

James: Did you look on the floor?

Maggie: Yes, I looked under my desk. The cards are not there.

Mrs. Lopez: Everyone, let's help Maggie search for her vocabulary cards. Please look on the floor around your desks.

Robert: I don't see them, Mrs. Lopez.

James: They are not under my desk. They have disappeared.

Mrs. Lopez: When was the last time you saw your vocabulary cards?

Maggie: I saw them just before Robert collected the magnets we used in our science experiment.

James: You said there was a big paper clip on your cards. I think I have solved the mystery. Robert, please get the magnets from the closet.

Mrs. Lopez: There are the missing cards! How did you know?

James: The paper clip must have stuck to the magnets. When Robert put the science supplies away, he didn't notice that he had Maggie's cards, too.

Maggie: I guess it was a case of attraction. The case is solved!

③

Reading Buddies (Grades 2-3)

Older readers, who may be reluctant to engage in enough repeated oral readings of text to develop fluency, will usually jump at the chance to read aloud to younger students. Arrange "reading buddy" partnerships between two classrooms. Pair up students in the older classroom with younger students who will be their regular reading buddies throughout the year. The older students visit the younger students' classroom and read books to their young friends.

1. In preparation for read-aloud sessions, encourage older readers to engage in several repeated readings of their books without an audience.

2. Instruct older readers to read the books aloud at least three times to a parent or an adult volunteer. Have the listeners sign their names on the **Reading Buddies Accountability Form (page 68)**.

3. Arrange a time for older readers to read the books to their reading buddies during read-aloud sessions.

4. Spend some time debriefing with older readers regarding fluency progress after read-aloud sessions.

Take It Home (Grades 1-3)

Form partnerships with parents early in the school year, so they can assist their children with repeated reading practice. Many teachers have seen their students realize enormous growth in oral reading fluency when parents worked as partners in achieving literacy goals.

1. Invite parents to school for a repeated-reading training session, in which you demonstrate how to do repeated readings and measure oral reading fluency.

2. Share research with parents that demonstrates the power of repeated readings. Use information from page 8, "Put It Into Practice."

3. Contract with parents to listen to 10 to 15 minutes of repeated readings three to five times per week. Ask them to sign the **Take It Home Accountability Form (page 68)** after each reading.

4. Make photocopies of the **Take It Home passages (pages 69-71)** for each student.

5. Ask parents to read aloud more challenging text to their children to model how the text should sound.

Reading Buddies

Accountability Form

Name: _____

I have enjoyed reading _____ (title of book).
I would like to read it to you. Please sign and date this form if I read my book to you.

Name   **Date**

1. _____   _____

2. _____   _____

3. _____   _____

I need to read my book *at least* three people.

Take It Home

Accountability Form

Name: _____

I want to become a fluent reader, so I need to read my reading passages aloud at least three times to a grown-up. Please sign below if I read my passage to you three times.

Week of: _____   **Week of:** _____

Monday: _____   Monday: _____

Tuesday: _____   Tuesday: _____

Wednesday: _____   Wednesday: _____

Thursday: _____   Thursday: _____

Friday: _____   Friday: _____

Take It Home

From Dairy to Glass

Milk is an important food. It helps build strong bones. It helps make teeth strong. Drinking milk gives you energy. Most milk in the market is from cows that live on a dairy farm. There are six main kinds of dairy cows. One breed is the Holstein. They are black and white. They produce the most milk.

A special machine milks the cows. They are milked twice a day. Cold, clean milk is kept in a tank. It is treated to be sure that it is healthy. Finally, the milk is put in cartons. Trucks deliver the fresh milk to your supermarket.

It is easy to have milk every day. You can drink it by the glass. Cheese and butter are made from milk. Ice cream and yogurt are made from milk, too.

Take It Home

The Fourth of July

Parade begins,
Drums go by.
We have fun
On the Fourth of July.

Bands march
Straight and tall.
I like the trumpets
Most of all.

Flags flutter
And touch the sky.
Banners wave
On the Fourth of July.

A man sells ice cream.
Tasty treat,
Frosty cold
In summer heat.

Sandwiches
And cookies, too,
Lemonade
For me and you.

Sun has set.
Here's the evening sky.
Time to look up
On the Fourth of July.

Fireworks crackle,
Fireworks bloom,
In glittering showers
And glowing plumes.

Red, white, and blue
Light up the sky.
We honor our nation
On the Fourth of July!

2

Take It Home

The New Wall

Peter crouched at the bottom of a hill on his family's farm. His father had given him a difficult job to do. He had asked Peter to move a large pile of rocks from the bottom of the hill to the top of the hill. The rocks were going to be materials for a new wall. Peter picked up a rock and held it in his hands. It was heavy. The job probably would take all day.

"Hello, Peter," his friend John said. "What are you doing?"

Peter had an idea. "I'm building up my strength," he answered.

"Why?" John asked.

"There is going to be a race at the county fair next week," Peter explained. He lifted the rock high over his head and lowered it again.

John nodded. "So? What has that got to do with picking up rocks?"

Peter looked left and right and then whispered the answer, "I'm carrying the rocks up the hill for exercise. I can feel my arms and legs getting stronger already. I know it will help me run faster, and I'll certainly win the race."

"That's a good idea," John answered. "Do you mind if I help?"

Peter smiled, "I guess that would be okay."

As the boys worked, another friend walked by. Soon he was carrying rocks, too. Before long, four boys were hard at work. They carried each rock up the hill and then trotted back down the hill to get another one. Within an hour, the pile of rocks had been moved.

"Thanks," John said before he left. "That was a good workout."

3

"It sure was," Peter answered with a grin.

Keeping Track (Grades 2–3)

This method of repeated reading involves students keeping track of their own oral reading fluency scores over a period of time. When students assess and monitor their own fluency, motivation increases.

1. Organize the class into pairs according to reading levels.

2. Select appropriately-leveled reading passages, such as the **Keeping Track passages (pages 75–76)** or other passages with cumulative word counts. A number of commercial programs have passages already marked, including *Great Leaps Reading Program* (Campbell, 1996, *www.greatleaps.com*) and *Read Naturally* (Ihnot, 2001, *www. readnaturally.com*).

3. Place the passages in plastic sheet protectors so students can mark the pages repeatedly.

4. Ask the first reader to read the passage aloud for one minute (signal the start and stop time). Instruct his or her partner to listen and circle any errors by marking on the plastic sheet protector with a wipe-off marker.

5. Show the pair how to work together to figure out the first reader's words correct per minute (words read minus errors) and mark it on the **Fluency Record Sheet reproducible (page 73)**.

6. Ask the second reader to read the passage aloud for one minute (signal the start and stop time), while his or her partner listens and circles any errors.

7. Prompt partners to work together to figure out the second reader's words correct per minute and mark the form.

Fluency Record Sheet

Week of: _____

Day 1   _____ words read correctly

Day 2   _____ words read correctly

Day 3   _____ words read correctly

Day 4   _____ words read correctly

Week of: _____

Day 1   _____ words read correctly

Day 2   _____ words read correctly

Day 3   _____ words read correctly

Day 4   _____ words read correctly

Week of: _____

Day 1   _____ words read correctly

Day 2   _____ words read correctly

Day 3   _____ words read correctly

Day 4   _____ words read correctly

Week of: _____

Day 1   _____ words read correctly

Day 2   _____ words read correctly

Day 3   _____ words read correctly

Day 4   _____ words read correctly

Tips on "Keeping Track"

DeeAnn Jamison, Second-Grade Teacher, Highlands Elementary, La Mesa, CA

I have seen tremendous growth in reading levels when using "Keeping Track" to develop reading fluency in my classroom. At the beginning of the school year, it takes second graders about 15 to 20 minutes to complete all the steps with multiple selections. As a teacher who needs to make every minute count, I motivate students to beat their time by offering an incentive. For example, if we better our time on task, students earn math, spelling, or vocabulary game time. Within two weeks, we are completing the process in about eight to ten minutes.

Managing students who squabble is done swiftly. After the first group of readers is finished reading the selection, I give the readers a chance to contest their score by rereading any circled words to me. If readers can correctly read the words to me, I give them credit. (It has been my experience that this process is quick and not overused by the class in general. Once in awhile, a pair does not get along, so I reassign them to other partners.) When each reader has written the word count on the record sheet in black ink, I give the signal for the recorder to wipe the marks off the sheet protector. Now the recorder becomes the reader and vice versa. We continue with each passage in the same manner.

In my second-grade class, we read each selection in the packet four times (Monday through Thursday). Most students enjoy being first, so if you are the second reader on Monday, you will be the first reader on Tuesday. One other modification I make is to offer to give the correct pronunciation and definition of any "tricky" word on Tuesday after we are finished reading. This is the midpoint of the time spent on each selection. The readers have had four previous opportunities to decode the selection by this point (two oral readings by each partner) and have four more opportunities to read the word properly over the next two days.

"Keeping Track" of repeated oral readings is truly a simple, systematic way to increase fluency in the primary classroom.

Name _____   Date _____

Keeping Track
Round and Round

Earth's water is on the move. It rises into the air, but it doesn't   (14)
keep going. Every drop goes around in a cycle. It is called the   (27)
water cycle. Most of our water is in the oceans. Some of it is   (41)
frozen in glaciers and icecaps. Some of it is fresh water in lakes   (54)
and rivers.   (56)

The sun starts the water cycle. It melts ice and warms water   (68)
in lakes and oceans. The water turns into a gas. It rises high in   (82)
the sky. The water does not get too far. It cools and turns back   (96)
into droplets. It forms clouds. If the air is very cold, the water   (109)
freezes. Clouds become too heavy to hold the water. Some falls   (120)
over the ocean as rain or snow. Sometimes rain or snow falls   (132)
over land. Some of the water soaks into the ground. It may travel   (145)
underground though soil and rocks. It can surface later as a pool   (157)
or spring. The rest of the water collects in lakes and rivers. This is   (171)
the last stage of the cycle. Rivers usually drain into the ocean. Then   (184)
the cycle starts all over again. We are lucky that the water cycle   (197)
works so well. Without water, nothing on Earth would survive.   (207)

Words Correct Per Minute: _____

Keeping Track

Daddy Longlegs

Daddy longlegs are not true spiders. They are more like spider (11)
cousins. They do not bite people, spin webs, or make nests. They (23)
live in fields and forests. Some live in houses with people. (34)

A daddy longlegs has a small, rounded body and a tiny dot (46)
on its head. On each side of the dot is a simple eye that can (61)
see movement. (63)

The daddy longlegs eats mites, spiders, and insects. Some also (73)
eat vegetable matter. (76)

This little creature is named for its eight very long legs. (87)
The second pair is the longest. If our legs were the same size (100)
compared to our body, they would be forty feet long! The daddy (112)
longlegs uses the sensitive second pair of legs to help it feel, (124)
smell, and taste. (127)

There are many kinds of daddy longlegs. Most die in winter. (138)
New ones hatch in spring. (143)

Words Correct Per Minute: _____

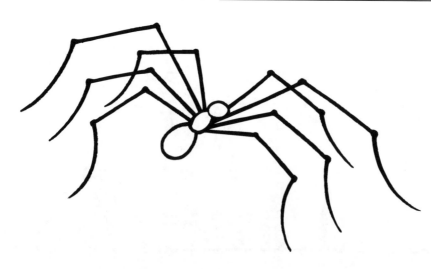

(3)

CHAPTER 6

Phrased Reading

Encourage Fluency Through Phrased Reading (Grades 1–2)

Besides being able to decode automatically, fluent readers chunk or parse text into syntactically appropriate units, mainly phrases (Rasinski, 2003). A dysfluent reader has great difficulty parsing or chunking text so that it makes sense. Practicing phrased reading should take place several times per week for about ten minutes per day.

Lesson 1

1. Give students copies of the **Phrased Reading passages (pages 78–80)**.

2. Read the segmented passage with appropriate intonation.

3. Have students read with you.

4. Have students practice reading together as a group. Provide feedback.

5. Have students read the passage aloud again.

Lesson 2

1. Read a segmented passage with appropriate intonation.

2. Have students read with you.

3. Have students read the segmented passage aloud in small groups and give each other feedback.

Lesson 3

1. Prompt students to read the segmented passage aloud as a group.

2. Have students read the segmented passage aloud in small groups and give each other feedback.

3. Repeat throughout the day.

Lesson 4

1. Distribute copies of the unsegmented passage.

2. Ask students to read the unsegmented passage aloud as a class.

3. Have students read the unsegmented passage in small groups. Provide feedback.

4. Prompt students to read the unsegmented passage aloud as a group.

Lesson 5

1. Meet with students individually to assess their reading of the unsegmented passage.

2. Note students' expression, pauses, and phrasing, and provide feedback.

Phrased Reading

A World of Bugs
(Segmented Passage)

What is a bug?
A bug may be
an insect.
An insect has
six legs.
An insect has
three main body parts.
Some insects
have wings.
Most insects
lay eggs.
Butterflies, ants, and bees
are all insects.

A World of Bugs
(Unsegmented Passage)

What is a bug? A bug may be an insect. An insect has six legs. An insect has three main body parts. Some insects have wings. Most insects lay eggs. Butterflies, ants, and bees are all insects.

1

Name _____ Date _____

Phrased Reading

Show and Tell Day
(Segmented Passage)

It is Show and Tell Day
at school.
Maria shares
her favorite book.
Maria's book is
about a funny dog.
Andy shares
his toy truck.
Andy's truck is
green and yellow.
Paul shares
his rock collection.
Paul has
eight big rocks.
He has
twelve small,
shiny rocks, too.

Rachel shares
her pet hamster.
The hamster is
named Buster.
Buster,
the hamster,
is brown and white.
He likes to eat
carrots and peanuts.
Paul gives Buster
a peanut.
The class enjoys
Show and Tell Day.
Buster enjoys it, too.

Phrased Reading

Show and Tell Day
(Unsegmented Passage)

It is Show and Tell Day at school. Maria shares her favorite book. Maria's book is about a funny dog. Andy shares his toy truck. Andy's truck is green and yellow. Paul shares his rock collection. Paul has eight big rocks. He has twelve small, shiny rocks, too. Rachel shares her pet hamster. The hamster is named Buster. Buster, the hamster, is brown and white. He likes to eat carrots and peanuts. Paul gives Buster a peanut. The class enjoys Show and Tell Day. Buster enjoys it, too.

2

CHAPTER 7

Assessing Fluency

How to Measure Reading Fluency

Oral reading fluency is measured by asking a student to read an appropriate passage about 150–250 words in length, depending on the grade level. Estimates of readability can be ascertained through readability formulas (Chall & Dale, 1995), classroom materials that have already been graded by a publisher, or a standardized measure of oral reading fluency (e.g., *The Multilevel Academic Skills Inventory,* Howell, Zucker, & Morehead, 1994) that contains several testing selections for each grade level. If you are using passages from your own curriculum materials, select those that have minimal dialogue and no unusual names or words. Testing for reading fluency can begin at the mid first-grade level.

1. Make two photocopies of the **Assessing Fluency passages (pages 84–95)** that are appropriate for the student's grade level. Give one copy to the student and keep one copy for yourself.

2. Use a stopwatch to time the student's reading.

3. Tell the student to begin reading. When one minute has passed, make a double-slash mark after the last word read and stop the student. Different tests use different scoring methods, but generally, omissions, insertions, and self-corrections are not counted as errors. Substitutions and incorrectly identified words are counted as errors.

4. The score that counts is the number of words read correctly in one minute. Subtract errors and substitutions from the total number of words to determine the number of words read correctly per minute.

5. Record the student's score on the **Assessing Reading Fluency Sheet reproducible (page 83)**.

Accepted Levels of Reading Fluency

Oral reading fluency is a combination of accuracy and rate. The fluency score is reported as words correct per minute. To consider either accuracy or rate by itself is a meaningless exercise. For example, students who make no errors but read very slowly have as little likelihood of comprehending what they read as students who read very quickly but guess at and misidentify many words. The minimum acceptable target oral reading fluency rates for instructional purposes vary by grade level and difficulty of the text. The chart below provides some general guidelines.

Grade Level Expectancy of Words Correct per Minute

Grade	Fall	Winter	Spring
1	--	52	60
2	53	73	82
3	79	107	115
4	99	115	118
5	105	129	134
6	115	132	140

Source: Adapted from Marston and Magnusson (1988) and Rasinski (2003).

Reading fluency rates continue to be an excellent indicator of reading proficiency, including comprehension ability, through sixth grade. Once a student has reached an oral reading fluency rate of 140 words correct per minute, however, the question of rate is moot. Faster at this point is not better. When students are able to read rapidly as well as accurately, they should then focus their attention on improving expression, voice projection, and clarity of speech in their oral reading.

Assessing Reading Fluency Sheet

Student's Name: _____

150
145
140
135
130
125
120
115
110
105
100
95
90
85
80
75
70
65
60
55
50

WORDS CORRECT PER MINUTE

DATE

Assessing Fluency
Super Soccer

I am on a soccer team. There are twelve boys and girls (12)
on my team. We are called the Gold Rush, because our (23)
uniforms are black and gold, and we are fast. The soccer (34)
ball is black and white. When you play soccer, you have (45)
to kick the ball. On the field, you can't touch the ball (57)
with your hands. A team gets points when they kick the (68)
ball into the net. I am the goalie. That means I stop the (81)
ball when the other team tries to kick it into the net. I can (95)
touch the ball with my hands. I catch it and throw it back (108)
onto the field. This season we have already won five (118)
games. I hope that we will be the soccer champions (128)
this year! (130)

Words Correct Per Minute: _____

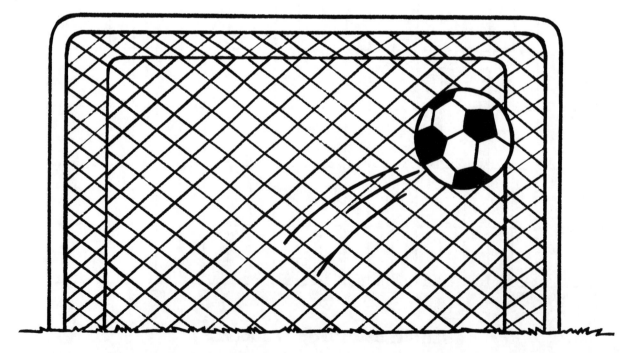

Mid
1

Assessing Fluency

My Music

    I love music. My mom says that I liked music before (11)
I could talk. I liked music before I could walk. She said (23)
she played music for me when I was a baby. I would (35)
smile. I would close my eyes. I would never cry when (46)
music played. We would sing together. We sang "Twinkle, (55)
Twinkle Little Star." We sang "Itsy Bitsy Spider." (63)

    Now I can play the piano. I play every day. I like the (76)
way the keys feel. First, I warm up. I play short pieces. (88)
Sometimes I sing. (91)

    Every time I play, I get a sticker. I put it in my notebook. (105)
When a page is full, I get a treat. I like to get strawberry (119)
ice cream. (121)

    My favorite song to play is called "A New Day." It is (133)
about a day with sunshine. It is about a day with a blue (146)
sky. It makes me happy. (151)

Words Correct Per Minute: _____

Mid
1

SEPTEMBER						
S	M	T	W	T	F	S
	1	2	3	4	5	6
7	8	9	10	11	12	13
14	15	16	17	18	19	20
21	22	23	24	25	26	27
28	29	30				

Assessing Fluency
Using the Calendar

There are twelve months in a year. A calendar shows (10)
each month. A calendar shows the weeks. There are (19)
about four weeks in a month. A calendar shows the (29)
days. There are seven days in a week. (37)

Calendars help us to remember special dates. You (45)
can circle your birthday on a calendar. You can circle (55)
the day that a friend will come to play. (64)

In school, the teacher picks a calendar helper. Each (73)
day the class names the day of the week. The first day (85)
of the school week is Monday. The last day of the school (97)
week is Friday. The helper circles the day. The helper (107)
changes the page when the month changes. The first (116)
month of the year is January. The last month of the year (128)
is December. (130)

There are four seasons in our calendar year. They are (140)
winter, spring, summer, and fall. Fall is when the leaves (150)
change. Winter is cold. Sometimes it snows. In spring, (159)
new flowers bloom. Summer is warm and sunny. (167)

We start each new school year in the fall. We have a (179)
winter break in December. We come back in January. (188)
We continue through spring. We do not go to school (198)
in the summer. Calendars are fun! (204)

Late
1

Words Correct Per Minute: _____

Assessing Fluency
Money in the Bank

Saving money is a good idea. I have a piggy bank. (11)
It has a slot in the top. When I earn money, I put it in my (27)
bank. To earn money I help with chores. I water plants for (39)
my mom. I sweep the porch for my dad. I rake leaves in (52)
the yard. I walk my neighbor's dog. (59)

Sometimes I get money for my birthday. I spend some. (69)
I put some in the piggy bank. Every week I open my (81)
bank and count the money. When I have enough, I put (92)
some in the real bank in a savings account. Each month (103)
the bank sends me a letter. It tells me how much money (115)
is in my account. (119)

The bank has a big safe with a heavy door. My money (131)
is not always in the safe. The bank lets other people (142)
borrow it. The bank pays to use my money. The money (153)
I earn is called interest. The money in my savings (163)
account grows. (165)

Someday I will use my money for something important. (174)
Maybe I will use it for a car. Maybe I will use it for college. (189)
I am glad I have a savings account. (197)

Words Correct Per Minute: _____

Late 1

Assessing Fluency

Our National Symbol

Look at the back of a quarter. You will see a bald eagle. This (14)
bird is our national symbol. The bald eagle stands for freedom. (25)
It stands for strength and bravery. (31)

The bald eagle is not really bald. It got its name from the white (45)
feathers on its head and tail. In old English, *bald* means "white." (57)
The body feathers are brown. It has a big, curved, yellow beak. (69)

Bald eagles live near water, like rivers and lakes. They eat fish (81)
and birds and other animals. They even eat dead animals. This is (93)
good because it helps to keep the land clean. (102)

Bald eagles can fly very fast. They can even swim. They lay (114)
about three eggs a year. Some bald eagles use the same nest for (127)
many years. They add twigs every year. The nest gets bigger and (139)
bigger. One old eagle nest weighed as much as an elephant! (150)

Words Correct Per Minute: _____

Early
2

Assessing Fluency

Amazing Plants

Life on earth depends on plants. Many animals eat plants.   (10)
People eat plants, too. They use parts of plants to make homes,   (22)
tools, and clothing. Plants do not have to find food. They make   (34)
their own food from the sun. Leaves are a plant's food factories. (46)
They use water, air, and sunshine to make food for the whole plant. (59)
The leaf can also breathe for the plant. Air and water move in and (73)
out through tiny openings under the leaves.   (80)

The stem supports the plant. Water and food travel through the   (91)
stem to all of the leaves and to the ends of the roots. Some plants (106)
have very special stem parts. They become tendrils, runners,   (115)
or thorns.   (117)

You usually can't see them at work, but the roots are a very   (130)
important part of most plants. Roots anchor the plant into the   (141)
ground. They soak up water. They soak in minerals from the soil.   (153)

Many plants have flowers. Flowers produce the seeds that grow   (163)
into new plants. In each seed there is the beginning of a new plant. (177)
The seed also holds food for the new plant. Seeds may spread by   (190)
wind or water. They may even be spread by animals.   (200)

Words Correct Per Minute: _____

Early
2

Assessing Fluency

Web Story

    Some spiders build webs, and some do not. The trapdoor spider (11)
does not build a web. It digs a burrow. Under its fangs it has (25)
spines. The spider uses its spines to scrape a hole in the ground. (38)
It lines its burrow with spider silk. The silk is made in the spider's (52)
body. It comes out through a hole in the underside of the spider. (65)

    The trapdoor spider makes a special lid of earth and leaves or (77)
grass. Some spiders build in escape routes or false doors. (87)

    The burrow protects the spider from rain. The spider stays in (98)
its burrow during the day. At night some spiders open the lid a (111)
little. Others hold the lid shut until they sense an insect. Hairs (123)
on the spider's legs help it to sense prey. The spider leaps out, (136)
snatches its victim, and quickly drags it into the burrow. (146)

    The water spider does build a web. It spins its web on plants (159)
that grow under water. It collects bubbles of air on its legs and (172)
body. It stores the bubbles under its web. This spider feeds on tiny (185)
water animals and fish. It hunts them under water. It stays under (197)
for a long time. The spider breathes in the air trapped in its web. (211)

    Words Correct Per Minute: _____

Late
2

Assessing Fluency

The Arctic Bear

The polar bear is one of the biggest bears in the world. It is up (15)
to eight feet long. It is up to five feet high at the shoulder. The (30)
polar bear lives in the Arctic. It spends a lot of its time along the (45)
coastline. It also spends time on the ice of the Arctic Sea. Polar (58)
bears are excellent swimmers. (62)

The polar bear hunts seals, walruses, and even some whales. (72)
It usually eats the blubber, not the meat. A single bear may eat (85)
one hundred pounds of blubber in one meal. It also eats fish. (97)
Sometimes it eats kelp, a large, leafy sea plant. (106)

A layer of blubber under its skin keeps the bear warm. The polar (119)
bear also has a thick fur coat. Each hair is hollow and colorless. (132)
The hair looks white because it reflects most light. The hairs allow (144)
some light rays in to the bear's charcoal black skin. Things that are (157)
black soak up and hold heat. Hair also covers the pads of the polar (171)
bear's huge paws. This gives the bear much better footing on the (183)
slippery ice. It also softens the sound of its footsteps. Polar bears (195)
rely on surprise in order to capture their prey. (204)

Words Correct Per Minute: _____

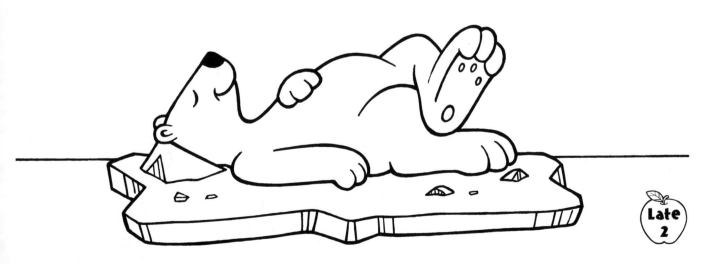

Late
2

Assessing Fluency

By the Sea

   Waves form when wind blows across open water. The size of a   (12)
wave depends on how fast, how long, and how far the wind blows.   (25)
When a wave nears a shallow shore, it slows down. Water at the   (38)
top of the wave starts moving faster than the water at the bottom.   (51)
The wave gets top-heavy and spills over. It becomes a foamy wave   (64)
along the shore.   (67)

   The shoreline is where the sea meets the land. Some shores are   (79)
sandy slopes. Others are rocky. At high tide, some rocks are under   (91)
water. At low tide, they are exposed.   (98)

   Seawater stays in pools between the rocks. The pools are home   (109)
to many living things. Sometimes the plants and animals are under   (120)
water, and sometimes they are in the hot sun. Kelp, sea urchins,   (132)
and sea stars live in tidepools by the sea.   (141)

Words Correct Per Minute: _____

Early
3

Assessing Fluency

Amazing Reptiles

How are snakes, lizards, turtles, and crocodiles alike? They (9)
all belong to a special animal group called reptiles. There are (20)
thousands of reptiles in the world. There are many different kinds (31)
of reptiles. What makes a reptile? It has a backbone. You have a (44)
backbone, too. A reptile breathes air through lungs. You breathe (54)
air through lungs, too. (58)

So, how are people and reptiles different? A reptile is cold- (69)
blooded. The blood of a reptile isn't really cold. Cold-blooded just (81)
means that body temperature is the same as the surroundings. (91)
When a reptile is too cold, it may bask in the sun to warm up. If it (108)
is too hot, it may find shade or go for a swim. (120)

Some snakes are born live, but most reptiles lay eggs. The (131)
leathery shell of a reptile's egg prevents it from drying out. Finally, (143)
most reptiles are covered by scales or hard plates. This helps to (155)
keep water in the animal's body. (161)

Most reptiles eat meat, insects, or eggs. Some, like the iguana, (172)
eat green plants. (175)

Reptiles have unique abilities. Some lizards can lose their tail (185)
and still escape from predators. They grow a new tail. Certain (196)
lizards can change color. Some turtles can live for more than one (208)
hundred years. Reptiles are amazing creatures. (214)

Words Correct Per Minute: _____

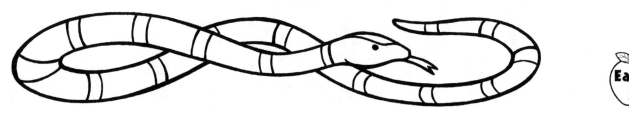

Early
3

Assessing Fluency

Life in the Treetops

How would you like to live in the treetops? Many rainforest (11)
animals do. Some insects, birds, and other animals never come to (22)
the ground. They eat leaves, fruit, nuts, and seeds. They live and (34)
hide among the leaves. One of the highest parts of the rainforest (46)
is called the canopy. The crowns of the trees grow close together. (58)
They form a treetop garden. The canopy may be ten stories above (70)
the ground. (72)

In the canopy, flowers bloom. The blossoms attract butterflies (81)
and hummingbirds that pollinate the flowers. Parrots, macaws, (89)
and bats eat fruits and nuts, such as the guava and Brazil nuts. (102)
The birds use their powerful curved beaks for crunching nuts and (113)
seeds. The bats sleep during the day. They hang upside down in (125)
the canopy. (127)

Hundreds of tiny animals live in the canopy, too. Many plants (138)
live among the tree branches. Water captured in the center of (149)
these plants is home to tree frogs, water beetles, and snails. Even (161)
lizards, mice, and earthworms live in the canopy. (169)

In some rainforests, spider monkeys swing in the treetops. (178)
The spider monkey hangs from its tail. The sloth doesn't swing. (189)
It hardly moves. It clings to branches with its sharp claws. The (201)
treetop canopy is filled with life. (207)

Words Correct Per Minute: _____

Late
3

Name _____ Date _____

Assessing Fluency

Unicorns

    The unicorn is an animal of myth. People of the Middle Ages (12)
said it was as white as new fallen snow. It looked like a beautiful (26)
horse with a long curly mane and tail. Sometimes it had a small (39)
white beard at the tip of its chin. The unicorn was a magic animal. (53)
Its magic was in a spiral horn in the middle of its forehead. Baby (67)
unicorns were born with a tiny star where the horn would grow. (79)

    The horn made dirty water fresh again. It was also a cure for (92)
poison. That is why people hunted unicorns. The unicorn was shy. (103)
It lived deep in the forest. It ate flowers instead of grass. It stayed (117)
away from humans. If it was in danger, it could run as fast as the (132)
wind. If a hunter cornered a unicorn, it would fight. (142)

    The unicorn was drawn to purity. If a nice young girl sat quietly (155)
among the trees, the unicorn would slowly come near. It would (166)
lay its head gently in her lap. (173)

    Unicorns may be a myth, but they are still popular. Today you (185)
can buy unicorn tee-shirts and posters. There are even books and (197)
movies about unicorns. (200)

Words Correct Per Minute: _____

Late 3

References

Allington, R. L. (1983). Fluency: The neglected goal. *The Reading Teacher, 36,* 556–561.

California Department of Education. (2001). *Criteria for 2002 language arts adoption.* Retrieved May 28, 2001, from http://www.cde.ca.gov/cilbranch/eltdiv/2002lacriteria.html.

Campbell, K. U. (1996). *Great leaps reading program.* Gainsville, FL: Diarmuid Inc.

Chall, J. S., & Dale, E. (1995). *Readability revisited: The new Dale-Chall readability formula.* Cambridge, MA: Brookline.

Dolch, E. W. (1948). *Problems in reading.* Champaign, IL: The Garrard Press.

Fry, E. (2004). *1,000 instant words by Dr. Fry.* Westminster, CA: Teacher Created Resources.

Fuchs, L. S., Fuchs, D., Hops, M. K., & Jenkins, J. R. (2001). Oral reading fluency as an indicator of reading competence: A theoretical, empirical, and historical analysis. *Scientific Studies of Reading, 5*(3), 239–245.

Gunning, T. G. (1998). *Assessing and correcting reading and writing difficulties.* Boston, MA: Allyn and Bacon.

Heckelman, R. G. (1969). A neurological-impress method of remedial reading instruction. *Academic Therapy, 4*(4), 277–282.

Howell, K. W., Zucker, S. H., & Morehead, M. K. (1994). *The multilevel academic skills inventory.* Paradise Valley, AZ: H & Z.

Ihnot, C. (2001). *Read naturally.* Retrieved June 23, 2007, from http://www.readnaturally.com.

Jenkins, J. R., Fuchs, L. S., Espin, C., van den Broek, P., & Deno, S. L. (2000, February). *Effects of task format and performance dimension on word reading measures: Criterion validity, sensitivity to impairment, and context facilitation.* Paper presented at Pacific Coast Research Conference, San Diego, CA.

Marston, D., & Magnusson, D. (1988). *Curriculum-based measurement: District level implementation.* Washington, DC: National Association of School Psychologists.

McEwan, E. K. (2002). *Teach them all to read: Catching the kids who fall through the cracks.* Thousand Oaks, CA: Corwin Press.

Mercer, C. D., & Campbell, K. U. (2001). *Great leaps.* Gainesville, FL: Diarmuid. Retrieved June 23, 2007, from http://www.greatleaps.com/default.asp.

National Reading Panel. (2002). *Report of the National Reading Panel: Teaching children to read: An evidence-based assessment of the scientific research literature on reading and its implications for reading instruction: Reports of the subgroups.* Rockville, MD: National Institute of Child Health and Human Development.

Opitz, M. E. &, Rasinski, T. V. (1998). *Good-bye round robin: 25 effective oral reading strategies.* Portsmouth, NH: Heinemann.

Rasinski, T. V. (2003). *The fluent reader.* New York, NY: Scholastic Professional Books.

Rasinski, T., Blachowicz, C., & Lems, K. (Eds.). (2006). *Fluency instruction: Research-based best practices.* New York, NY: The Guilford Press.

Searfoss, L. (1975). Radio reading. *The Reading Teacher, 29,* 295–296.

Shefelbine, J. (1999). Reading voluminously and voluntarily. In *Scholastic Reading Counts Research.* New York, NY: Scholastic. Retrieved June 12, 1999, from http://apps.scholastic.com/readingcounts/research/voluminouslky/voluntarily.

Sitton, R. (2002). *Rebecca Sitton's spelling sourcebook for eighth grade teachers.* Scottsdale, AZ: Eggers Publishing, Inc.

Snow, C. E., Burns, M. S., & Griffin, P. (Eds.). (1998). *Preventing reading difficulties in young children.* Washington, DC: National Academy Press, Committee on the Prevention of Reading Difficulties in Young Children, Commission on Behavioral and Social Sciences and Education, National Research Council.

Tompkins, G. (1998). *Fifty literacy strategies step by step.* Upper Saddle River, NJ: Merrill.

Trelease, J. (2006). *The read-aloud handbook.* New York, NY: Penguin Books.

Wolfe, P. (2001). *Brain matters: Translating research into classroom practice.* Alexandria, VA: Association for Supervision and Curriculum Development.

Printed in the United States
By Bookmasters